CW00920399

chocolate
magic

Kate Shirazi

Photography by Lara Holmes

PAVILION

First published in the United Kingdom in 2010 by
Pavilion Books
Old West London Magistrates Court
10 Southcombe Street
London, W14 0RA

An imprint of Anova Books Company Ltd

Design and layout © Pavilion, 2010
Text © Kate Shirazi, 2010
Photography © Lara Holmes, 2010

The moral right of the author has been asserted.

Commissioning editor: Emily Preece-Morrison
Designer: Georgina Hewitt
Photography: Lara Holmes, except images on pp. 9 and 82 by
Charlotte Barton and pp. 4, 11 and 29 by Yuki Sugiura
Food stylist: Monaz Dumasia
Prop stylist: Emily Preece-Morrison
Copy editor: Caroline Curtis
Indexer: Patricia Hymans

ISBN 978-1-86205-881-1

A CIP catalogue record for this book is available from the British Library.

10 9 8 7 6 5 4 3 2

Reproduction by Dot Gradations Ltd, United Kingdom
Printed and bound by Toppan Leefung Printing Ltd, China

www.anovabooks.com

Contents

Introduction

Oh, dear! Have you had a bad day? What do you mean, "No, it's been fine, thank you very much"? Look into my eyes – I think you've had a bad day and need something a little bit chocolatey to cheer you up. I'm right, aren't I? Your day has been truly terrible, hasn't it? Well, I'm here to make things better.

But good day or bad, you jolly well do need something with a smidgen of chocolate. As a very fine judge of character, I never completely trust a person who does not like chocolate. You do know what I mean. There is something inherently a bit odd about someone who doesn't relish the unctuous gorgeousness of a bit of lovely, lovely chocolate melting in the mouth. For heaven's sake, even my dog loves chocolate.

(By the way, dogs should not be encouraged to adore chocolate. It is poison to them. Poor creatures. Greedy old Ted discovered my stash of Christmas chocolate and one night scoffed the lot. This included a bar of 70% chocolate with chilli. He thought it excellent. A box of champagne truffles was also excellent. As was a packet of chocolate biscuits. For those who are concerned, the dog is fine and the vet is richer.)

Chocolate is extraordinarily versatile. You can eat it in bar form or use it grated, melted, chopped or powdered, and it ranges from face-screwingly bitter to eyebrow-raisingly sweet. There's nothing quite like the expression on a baby's face when they taste their first bit of chocolate. For a nine-month-old (or however long you have managed to leave it before giving in), this is the holy grail.

The Aztecs, who knew a thing or two about chocolate, considered it an aphrodisiac and banned women from eating it, for fear of unleashing all sorts of frightening female fancifulness. Can you imagine banning women from chocolate these days? Oh my word! The wrath. The united power of millions of women, joining forces and demanding their chocolate rights from a load of men, sitting nibbling at their own, manly chocolate bars ...

The science bit

There is some science behind our love affair with chocolate. It contains theobromine – a stimulant that causes a lasting improvement in mood. It increases serotonin, endorphin and dopamine levels (the happy hormones), and acts as a mild anti-depressant, with a hint of stimulant thrown in for good measure. No wonder we love it so! I find it interesting (though others may not share this particular fascination) that the words "theobromine", "serotonin" and "dopamine" sort of roll round your mouth and tumble out in lovely round sounds. The word "ugly" *is* ugly and clunky. "Theobromine" is a beautiful, comforting word. Maybe I am taking this all a bit seriously now ... but before you write me off completely, here's another thing: cocoa butter melts at just below body temperature, which is why it dissolves so gorgeously in the mouth. What more evidence do you want? Humans are *meant* to eat chocolate. And I haven't even gone down the "it-contains-iron-and-calcium-and-all-sorts-of-other-goodies" route.

What to buy

You have probably heard many times before that what you cook will be only as good as the ingredients you use. Silk purse, sow's ear and all that. I have to say that this is very relevant to these recipes, *but* – you are under no obligation to buy only the finest single estate 72% chocolate, harvested by a man called Eric. Yes, you get what you pay for, but buy what you can afford and whatever strikes you as the best choice at the time. I am sure that a pudding made with single estate chocolate will taste better than a pudding made with cheap chocolate. But unless you are comparing and contrasting the two puddings, the one made with cheap chocolate will still taste good. It just won't be ambrosial.

A serious point to consider when buying chocolate is the issue of Fair Trade. Now, I really don't want to rant and make you, dear reader, feel uncomfortable and guilty. We do need to be aware, however, that the business of chocolate is often the cause of hideous injustice for the cacao farmers. There are plenty of Fair Trade chocolate brands available now. These are not difficult to find, and I reckon that the chocolate really does taste better. The finish is generally smoother. Yes, they are more expensive. I am happy to pay the extra because I see chocolate as a treat, not an everyday food, and I'm not thrilled at the thought of the farmer being ripped off. Up to you.

There is something else that nags at me, though: the issue of eggs. You will have seen that a donation from the sale of this book goes to The Battery Hen Welfare Trust. My garden is full of delightful, though destructive, hens. They are re-homed battery hens. This means that when I get them, they are straight out of a cage, never having set foot outside. They look hideous: very few feathers; huge, almost white combs; and mad, staring eyes. They don't really know what to do at first but then, magically, they get the hang of it. Fresh air. Proper space. Running, flapping, chasing, pecking and – joy of joys – dust baths. There is nothing better than watching a hen have her first dust bath. Believe me, these girls show a garden no respect, but although they are terrific vandals, they lay proper eggs (sometimes even deigning to lay them in the hen house and not in a hedge) and are curiously good company. Hens aren't meant to live in cages. Please buy free-range eggs. *Please.*

Cocoa

The one ingredient I do get very bossy about is cocoa. Cocoa and drinking chocolate are not the same. If a recipe says cocoa – for goodness' sake, use it. If you use drinking chocolate, you will be adding dried milk powder, sugar, all sorts of weird fats, and salt – and the recipe will not work. The only thing you may substitute for cocoa powder (unsweetened cocoa) is finely grated 100% cacao, which is utterly fantastic.

Melting chocolate

A word here is needed about melting chocolate. A lot of the recipes require chocolate to be used in its heavenly liquid form. There are two methods of melting chocolate (three, if you count giving it to a child to hold in the back of a car).

The first is the safest! Place the chopped-up chocolate in a heatproof bowl over a saucepan of barely simmering water. The crucial thing here is that the bottom of the bowl must not touch the water; the chocolate gets too hot. Nightmare: grainy ghastly mess; straight in the bin; tears. Don't do it.

The second method is quicker, more gung-ho, and I like to think of it as the rapid-assault method of melting chocolate. Quick, brutal – but not without risk: the microwave. Put the chopped chocolate into a microwaveable container, then zap it. Do short bursts of only 10–15 seconds and stir between each zapping. I recommend you stop while there are still some lumps and just keep stirring – the residual heat will melt the rest. The danger here is going for the burn (especially with white chocolate): one second, it is fine and dandy and thoroughly enjoying its little warm-up; the next second, Whoa! All gone horribly, horribly wrong. Have you ever tasted burnt chocolate? Nasty.

The recipes

The recipes in this book are meant to bring you joy, not drive you to distraction. If a recipe says it is easy, I mean it. It is. If I confess that it's a bit of a fiddle, it means that I have found it a bit of a fiddle – whether technically or because it took up time. What I am trying to say is that chocolate can be well behaved or it can need a bit of coaxing. There are recipes to suit those who can't be bothered to spend more than 10 minutes in the kitchen (fudge, popcorn, cookies, martinis ...) and for those who don't mind dedicating a rather extraordinarily great expanse of their life to a project like chocolate buns. There are, of course, loads of recipes that fall somewhere in between.

When I cook, I find it difficult to follow recipes exactly. Some people prefer to follow recipes to the letter, and others have a rather more "freestyle" approach, flinging in alternative ingredients, snorting and tutting over methods and timings. I'll be as thrilled by either approach towards this book. Add, subtract, alter and embellish – I think that's what recipes should be all about. On the other hand, if you prefer to follow a recipe religiously, these recipes do work, so make your choice! That said, if you are going for the strict approach, please be aware that your oven will cook rather differently to mine, and timings in particular are a guide only. Some people prefer plain (bittersweet) chocolate to milk, and vice versa – if a recipe insists you use one, you needn't; substitute with your choice. The resulting texture may be a bit different, but does it matter if it tastes just how you like it?

Now, I'll stop being bossy (for a moment, anyway). And just add that I hope you enjoy the book and make something truly deliciously chocolatey – and that your day gets much, much better ...

Little treats 1

Picture this event from my childhood. I was having a sleep-over with one of my best chums. Her parents were like Margot and Jerry from *The Good Life*. My friend's mother had taken to her bed early in the evening. We were invited to join her for a chat, and there she was, wearing an extraordinarily elaborate bed jacket, surrounded by magazines, tissues, nail varnish and the most massive box of chocolates you have ever seen. She was wallowing in bed, popping chocolates into her mouth. Barbara Cartland couldn't have done better. We perched on the end of the bed and had a chat about school and ponies and other important issues, while she worked her way through the chocolates. Absolutely fabulous. Looking back on this remarkable event, I think she was having a bad day and knew how to sort herself out. Take to your bed with chocolate. Who on earth could argue with that?

Now, the really great thing about this first chapter is that a high percentage of these little choccies, sweets and treats take just moments to make and require no skill. In fact, some are embarrassingly easy. Taking a box of homemade chocolates to a friend's house is brilliant, especially if you find a really pretty box to put them in. These are seriously delicious and can be presented with a flourish of pride. Yum.

Your basic truffle

Truffles are so easy to make, it's a shame not to rustle some up at every opportunity. This is the basic recipe, which can be added to at will. Chuck stuff in like nuts, dried fruits, a slug of alcohol, a smidgen of chilli (really, I'm not joking) – let your imagination run riot. These work just as well with milk, plain (bittersweet) or white chocolate. The only thing you might notice is that with some chocolate you have to wait a little longer for the ganache to firm up before you can form it.

✱ Makes about 30 (but this does depend on whether you are going for golf balls or marbles)

100 g/3½ oz/3½ squares chocolate
100 ml/3½ fl oz/scant ½ cup double (heavy) cream
about 2 tbsp cocoa powder (unsweetened cocoa)

Smash the chocolate up into gravelly chunks – bash it with a rolling pin or pulse it in a food processor. I have found breaking it with your hands unsatisfactory; too much ends up in your mouth.

To make the ganache, gently heat the cream to just below boiling point and then take it off the heat. Throw in the chopped chocolate and stir gently until all the chocolate has melted. Leave the ganache to firm up for at least 30 minutes; the timing will depend on which chocolate you have used.

When the mixture has firmed up, line a large baking sheet with greaseproof (waxed) paper and sprinkle a thin layer of cocoa powder (unsweetened cocoa) onto the paper. Take small teaspoons of the mixture and form into balls – either with your hands, or using a couple of spoons. Then roll the truffle through the cocoa and leave it there. When you have used up all the mixture, place the baking sheet of truffles in the refrigerator for at least 2 hours.

Finally, pack into pretty boxes and delight someone.

Midas truffles

These aren't what you might call "value truffles". I would go so far as to say that these are full-on, luxury truffles. And I don't joke when I call them Midas Truffles. They are covered in edible gold leaf. Real gold, getting really scoffed. Brilliant! So, for goodness' sake, don't go and spoil it all by using nasty chocolate with a really low cocoa content. Go for broke – you are going to be anyway. Incidentally, silver leaf works just as well.

* Makes about 12

50 ml/2 fl oz/¼ cup double (heavy) cream
50 g/1¾ oz/1¾ squares best quality plain (bittersweet) chocolate, chopped
4 sheets of edible gold leaf

* *You will find these pictured on p.11.*

* TOP TIP:
You will need a very soft brush, preferably flat edged.

First prepare the ganache. Heat the cream to just below boiling point and then take it off the heat. Add the chocolate and stir gently until it has all melted, then leave the ganache to set.

Take small teaspoons of the mixture and form into balls. Place on a plate and then pop the plate of naked truffles in the refrigerator for 20 minutes, or until firm.

Shut all the windows and doors. Exclude any draughts and threaten with pain of death anyone who tries to create even the faintest movement of air around you. Open up the gold leaf and carefully tear a little piece off and place it on the truffle. Then carefully brush it into place. The gold will cling to the truffle and stay there. Carry on until the whole truffle is covered. I like to have tiny gaps between the chocolate and gold. I think they look better this way – not so "foil covered". They will keep well in the refrigerator for at least 3 days.

For an economy version, make the truffles as above, but instead of letting them set in the refrigerator, put them onto a plate liberally sprinkled with edible golden glitter. Give the plate a shake to roll the truffle all the way through the glitter, and you're done.

Champagne truffles

A decadent treat: rich, alcoholic, extravagant, and pretty. What's more, you've had to open a bottle of champagne and there's quite a lot left over. Seems a shame to waste it ...

✳ Makes about 30

100 g/3½ oz/3½ squares plain (bittersweet) chocolate, smashed into gravel-size chunks
100 g/3½ oz/3½ squares milk chocolate, smashed into gravel-size chunks
150 ml/5 fl oz/⅔ cup double (heavy) cream
4 tbsp champagne
1 tbsp brandy

For the coating
200 g/7 oz/7 squares milk chocolate
8 amaretti biscuits (cookies), crushed to a fine powder

Put the smashed chocolate into a heatproof bowl. Heat the cream to just below boiling point and pour over the chocolate. Stir gently until all the chocolate has melted, then stir in the champagne and the brandy. Put the bowl into the refrigerator and leave for at least 1 hour, or until set; this will make the mixture easier to handle.

Remove the chocolate mixture from the refrigerator. Using a melon baller, gouge balls of the truffle mixture out of the bowl and pop them on a baking sheet lined with greaseproof (waxed) paper. You can use your hands, but it does get very messy and the finished shapes aren't quite as good.

Put the tray of truffles back into the refrigerator to re-set.

Meanwhile, melt the milk chocolate and pour into a shallow dish. Pour the powdered amaretti biscuits (cookies) into a shallow dish. Lay out another sheet of greaseproof paper on another baking sheet.

Take the truffles out of the refrigerator. Using a truffle fork or a couple of teaspoons, roll a truffle first in the melted chocolate and then straight through the amaretti powder, and then set down on the greaseproof paper. Continue until all the truffles are coated, then return them to the refrigerator for 2 hours, or until you choose to pop them into petit four cases, a pretty box, or your own mouth.

Chocolate fudge

This chocolatey, sublimely smooth fudge is spookily easy. I have had all sorts of trouble with fudge in the past. Terrible boiling issues and endless trials on cold saucers and blobs in glasses of water ... all too complicated for me – and too much like hard work. And more often than not, the results aren't worth the effort. This recipe requires no boiling, no testing, just a bit of mild stirring – and *voilà*! Line the baking sheet with the miracle that is re-useable silicone liners. It will make getting the fudge out of the tin (pan) an absolute doddle. A word of warning: don't cut the fudge while it is still on the liner – you will cut the silicone.

✳ Makes about 60 pieces

200 g/7 oz/7 squares plain (bittersweet) chocolate
200 g/7 oz/7 squares milk chocolate
400 g/14 oz tin (can) condensed milk
3 tsp vanilla extract

Use silicone liner or good-quality greaseproof (waxed) paper to line a tin (pan) that measures about 20 cm/8 in square (the measurement needn't be exact). Break up the chocolate and place in a heatproof bowl with the condensed milk. Put the bowl over a pan of barely simmering water, making sure that the bottom of the bowl doesn't touch the water.

Heat until all the chocolate is melted, stirring pretty constantly. Then take it off the heat and beat in the vanilla.

Pour into the lined tin and smooth out the fudge. Put it in the refrigerator for at least 2 hours, or overnight.

Lift the plank of fudge out of the tin and remove the liner. Using a sharp knife, cut the fudge into little squares. This can then be bagged up and thrust into eager hands – or kept in the refrigerator for up to 2 weeks.

Chocolate prunes

Oh my word, I love these things! The combination of soft, sweet and slightly alcoholic prune, crunchy almond and dark, almost bitter, crisp chocolate is just lovely. And they're criminally easy to make. Use the plumpest, softest prunes you can find. And use a top-quality plain (bittersweet) chocolate; with this recipe, it really does pay.

* Makes about 24

250 ml/9 fl oz/1 cup freshly made Earl Grey tea
150 ml/5 fl oz/⅔ cup port
24 ready-to-eat (no-soak) prunes
24 blanched whole almonds
200 g/7 oz/7 squares plain (bittersweet) chocolate (70–72% cocoa solids)

Place the hot tea and the port in a bowl and pop the prunes into their lovely bath. Leave for at least 30 minutes, but the longer, the better.

Remove the prunes and place on some paper towel to absorb excess bathing liquids. Pop an almond inside each prune.

Melt the plain (bittersweet) chocolate and place a sheet of greaseproof (waxed) paper or some silicone liner onto a baking sheet.

Spear a prune with a cocktail stick (toothpick) and dunk it into the chocolate. You might need to use a teaspoon to dribble melted chocolate all over the prune. When well covered, place on the baking sheet. Continue until all the prunes are covered, then leave them to set.

When the chocolate has hardened, peel the prunes off the baking paper and place them in petit four cases. Delicious.

White chocolate and coconut nibbles

Those die-hard fans of white chocolate (and there are many) just adore these. Yes, Deborah, I am talking about you ... The one thing to remember is that you must not use desiccated (dry unsweetened) coconut. Use shavings of dried coconut, which can be found in all health food shops. It is a lovely combination: creamy white chocolate and nutty toasted coconut – and criminally easy, but you needn't tell anyone.

✳ Makes about 20

250 g/9 oz coconut shavings
350 g/12 oz/12 squares white
   chocolate, chopped
200 ml/7 fl oz/generous ¾ cup
   double (heavy) cream
1 tsp vanilla extract

First, spread the coconut onto a large baking sheet and pop under the grill (broiler) to toast. Watch it like a hawk: the coconut goes from pale to golden to black in the blink of an eye. When golden, remove and leave to cool.

Melt the white chocolate in a heatproof bowl over a pan of simmering water, remembering not to let the bottom of the bowl touch the water.

Take the chocolate off the heat and quickly beat in the cream. Add the vanilla and beat well again. Add the coconut and stir in carefully.

Pop teaspoons of the mixture into petit four cases and leave them in the refrigerator to set. *Voilà*.

Chocolate peanut butter cups

If you love the mix of salty and sweet, crunchy and smooth, then you will love these. They are not sophisticated in any way, shape or form. Like hot dogs, candy floss and marshmallows, these are something you won't want all the time, but you'll find them delicious every now and then. They also look like they should be tricky, but they aren't.

*Makes about 10

250 g/9 oz/9 squares milk
   chocolate
2 rounded tsp white vegetable fat
2 tbsp crunchy peanut butter
2 tbsp icing (confectioner's)
   sugar, sifted
1 tsp vanilla extract
petit four cases or
   small cupcake cases

Melt the chocolate and the vegetable fat together in a heatproof bowl over a pan of barely simmering water, ensuring that the bottom of the bowl doesn't touch the water. Brush the melted chocolate inside the baking cases and place in the refrigerator to set – you should still have quite a bit of chocolate mixture left over. Repeat once more.

Put the peanut butter into a bowl and add the icing (confectioner's) sugar and vanilla. Beat it all together until you get a mixture stiff enough to form into little balls. If your peanut butter is quite runny, you may need to add more sugar until you get the right consistency.

When the chocolate cups have set, take little balls of the peanut butter mixture and pop them into the cases and squish them in a little.

Take teaspoons of the remaining melted chocolate and drizzle over the top of the peanut butter to completely seal the cups. Return to the refrigerator to harden.

Chocolate fruit & nut bites

Right. This recipe is so easy; the most you'll have to do is stir. The results, though, are scrumptious. You can use plain (bittersweet) or milk chocolate and whichever fruit and nuts you like. I think you do need fruit and nuts, but if you don't like prunes, don't use them. And if you want Brazil nuts? Shove them in.

✳ Makes about 20

50 g/1¾ oz/scant ¼ cup ready-to-eat (no-soak) prunes, chopped roughly
50 g/1¾ oz/scant ⅓ cup plump raisins
50 g/1¾ oz/¼ cup glacé (candied) cherries, chopped roughly
50 g/1¾ oz/⅓ cup whole blanched almonds
50 g/1¾ oz/⅓ cup whole toasted hazelnuts
200 g/7 oz/7 squares chocolate

Put the fruit and whole nuts into a large bowl. Melt the chocolate according to your preferred method, then pour over the fruit and nuts. Stir it all up and pop teaspoons of the mixture into petit four cases and leave to set. That's it.

If you are feeling very adult and wanton, you could think ahead and soak the dried fruit in alcohol before adding the nuts and chocolate.

Chocolate nut caramels

I feel I should make a small apology here. These are delicious and really worth making, but you need only a bit of the base caramel, which means you will be left with a whole bowl of gorgeous caramel. But there are uses for it! If you don't want to make Millionaire's Shortbread straight away (p.97) it keeps very happily in a jar in the refrigerator for weeks on end. It is lovely on ice cream and also sandwiched between plain, buttery biscuits. I have specified hazelnuts in the recipe, but any nut will do.

* Makes about 24

1 x 400 g/14 oz tin (can) condensed milk
175 g/6 oz/1½ sticks butter
175 g/6 oz/scant 1 cup caster (superfine) sugar
4 tbsp golden (corn) syrup
100 g/3½ oz/3½ squares milk chocolate
100 g/3½ oz/⅔ cup hazelnuts, toasted and chopped roughly
2 tbsp double (heavy) cream

First make the caramel by putting the condensed milk, butter, sugar and syrup into a big, heavy pan and heat gently until everything is melted and runny. Simmer gently for 5 minutes, stirring all the time, until the mixture becomes thick and golden. (Watch out for splashes and volcanic eruptions.) Remove from the heat and allow to cool slightly. Then transfer the caramel to a large jar or suitable container.

Take two generous tablespoons of the caramel and put into a heatproof bowl. Add the chopped chocolate and place the bowl over a bowl of barely simmering water. Don't let the water touch the bottom of the bowl. Once the chocolate has melted into the caramel, stir in the nuts and the cream.

Take the mixture off the heat and pop teaspoons of the caramel into petit four cases. Leave in the refrigerator to set.

Chocolate popcorn

This stuff is a hoot! And if your heart sinks at the idea of letting the children in the kitchen and having to deal with the mess and kerfuffle and eternity of it all – never fear! This is the recipe for you. It's all over in 10 minutes, and very little mess is involved. It doesn't keep well, so you'll have to eat it all straight away. Sorry. For fewer than four people, I'd halve the quantity.

✳ Makes a big bowlful

1 batch sticky chocolate sauce
    (see p.109),
2 tsp sunflower (corn) oil
90 g/3¼ oz/½ cup popping corn

First of all, preheat the oven to 180˚C/350˚F/Gas Mark 4 and line a big baking sheet with silicone liner or greaseproof (waxed) paper.

Warm the sticky chocolate sauce.

Pour the oil into a very large saucepan (one that has a close-fitting lid) and heat until the oil is quivering and shimmering. Add the popping corn and immediately put the lid on.

Shake the pan, holding the lid firmly on and keeping the pan on the heat. Go on, give it a good old shake. Keep on shaking. You will hear a "pop", then another, then another – and all of a sudden there will be a long, impressive volley of pops. Keep shaking that pan until the pops eventually stop.

Take off the lid and pour the chocolate sauce over the popcorn. Stir so that all the corn is covered in the sauce and then pour the whole lot onto the lined baking sheet. Spread it out well and then place the baking sheet in the oven for about 3 minutes. If you smell burning sugar, get it out quick! Leave it to cool.

When it is cold, you should have lovely chocolatey, crispy popcorn chunks. Dee-licious!

Liberty Florentines

I've taken liberties with this recipe! Traditionally, Florentines contain almonds (yum), raisins (yum), cherries (yum) and mixed peel (yuck). I can't make something with an ingredient that makes me want to wipe my tongue, so changes had to be made. And then I got all carried away and tropical...

✳ Makes 18–20

100 g/3½ oz/⅔ cup flaked (slivered) almonds
25 g/1 oz/¼ cup crystallized (candied) papaya
25 g/1 oz/¼ cup crystallized (candied) pineapple
25 g/1 oz/¼ cup crystallized (candied) ginger
25 g/1 oz/¼ cup glacé (candied) cherries
90 g/3¼ oz/generous ¾ stick butter
100 g/3½ oz/½ cup caster (superfine) sugar
50 g/2 oz/¼ cup plain (all-purpose) flour
1 tbsp double (heavy) cream
200 g/7 oz/7 squares chocolate, according to preference

Line three baking sheets with washable silicone liners or good-quality greaseproof (waxed) paper. Preheat the oven to 180°C/350°F/Gas Mark 4.

Roughly chop the almonds and the fruit. Melt the butter and the sugar over a low heat in a heavy-based pan. Turn up the heat and boil vigorously for 1 minute, stirring now and then. Remove from the heat and cool. Stir in the flour, then the cream, followed by the chopped fruit and nuts. Stir to combine.

Take small teaspoonfuls of the mixture and plop onto the baking sheets, leaving plenty of space between them. (I tell you, these babies spread.) Bake for 10 minutes, or until golden brown.

Remove from the oven. If you don't like the shape, take a spatula and push the sides around the Florentine to neaten. Leave alone on the tray for about 5 minutes to start firming up, then lift onto a wire rack to cool completely.

Melt your chocolate according to your preferred method, then leave to cool for about 10 minutes. Just as it is starting to thicken and is less runny, take a palette knife and spread the base of the Florentines with the chocolate, then place back onto the baking sheet to set, with the chocolate side up.

Desserts

2

Are there really any people out there who
don't like chocolate desserts and puddings?
After a delicious meal, you might think you
are full, and then someone mentions a tiny
hazelnut and chocolate meringue or a sliver
of chocolate roulade ...

In this chapter, I have tried to assemble
a variety of desserts. Some are solid and
heavy: winter warmers like chocolate
steamed pudding (p.33) or chocolate bread
and butter pudding (p.36). Others are light,
delicate and, dare I say it, sophisticated: a
white chocolate panna cotta (p.50) or
a chocolate chestnut terrine (p.48) makes a
good finish to a supper that has been more
fillets of sole than bangers and mash. As a
foil to the sophisticates, though, I have put in
a good dollop of kitsch. You can't beat a good
trifle, a sundae or a cheesecake. You can
pretend you are being ironic if you want, but
you and I both know that you have made
them because you want to eat them ...

Big-bottomed cheesecake

If you eat a lot of this, I can guarantee you will get a big bottom. I tried making it with low-fat dairy products, and it just isn't the same. Having said that, it is utterly delicious as a treat, to be shared with many people.

✳ Serves at least 12

For the base
150 g/5½ oz chocolate digestive biscuits, crushed
25 g/1 oz/¼ stick butter, melted
1½ tsp cocoa powder (unsweetened cocoa)

For the cheesecake
175 g/6 oz/scant 1 cup caster (superfine) sugar
600 g/1 lb 5 oz/generous 2½ cups cream cheese
1 vanilla pod (bean)
375 ml/13 fl oz/generous 1½ cups double (heavy) cream
175 g/6 oz crème fraîche (sour cream)
200 g/7 oz fromage frais
2 tbsp lemon juice
1 tsp vanilla extract
100 g/3½ oz/generous ½ cup chocolate chips

For the topping
100 ml/3½ fl oz/scant ½ cup double (heavy) cream
100 g/3½ oz/3½ squares plain (bittersweet) chocolate

✳ *You will need a deep, non-stick, 20 cm/8 in diameter cake tin (pan), with a removable base*

Mix the crushed biscuits, butter and cocoa together, then put into the bottom of the tin (pan) and press down well. Put it in the refrigerator to chill. For a firmer base, bake for 5–8 minutes at 180°C/350°F/Gas Mark 4 before putting in the refrigerator.

In a large bowl, mix together the sugar, cream cheese and seeds scraped from the vanilla pod (bean).

In another large bowl, whisk together the cream, crème fraîche, fromage frais, lemon juice and vanilla extract until you get to the soft peak stage. Fold this into the cream cheese mixture, followed by the chocolate chips. Taste, and add more lemon juice or vanilla if necessary.

Tip the whole lot onto the base and smooth the top. Place back in the refrigerator for at least 4 hours, or overnight.

To make the topping, heat the cream to just below boiling point. Break the chocolate into pieces, place in a bowl, then pour in the cream and stir until the chocolate has all melted. Leave to cool and thicken slightly, then pour over the cheesecake. Chill again, for at least 1 hour.

Just before serving, run a knife around the edge of the tin and push the base up. It usually behaves incredibly well. I leave it on the base and put the whole lot onto the serving plate, but remove the base too if you want.

Baked chocolate cheesecake

My friend Gretchen is a wonderful cook who runs a cookery school. She taught me to make a fabulous baked cheesecake, and that got me thinking. Always dangerous. In a ruthless and shameful manner, I have taken her recipe and turned it into a chocolate version of her original. Gretchen: thank you and sorry.

✳ Serves 12

100 g/3½ oz/3½ squares plain (bittersweet) chocolate
50 g/1¾ oz/⅓ cup plain (all-purpose) flour, sifted, plus some for the tin (pan)
200 g/7 oz/1 cup caster (superfine) sugar
1 tbsp cocoa powder (unsweetened cocoa)
pinch of salt
1 kg/2 lb 4 oz ricotta cheese
6 large eggs, lightly beaten
2 tsp vanilla extract
grated zest of 2 large oranges

Preheat the oven to 160°C/325°F/Gas Mark 3. Butter and flour a 23 cm/9 in springform cake tin (pan). Melt the chocolate according to your preferred method and leave to cool.

In a bowl, mix together the flour, sugar, cocoa and salt.

In another bowl, beat the ricotta till smooth and then gradually add the eggs. After they are all incorporated, whisk in the chocolate. Add the flour mixture and mix thoroughly, then pour into the prepared tin and pop the tin onto a baking sheet. Bake for 1 hour 20 minutes, or until a skewer comes out cleanly. Let it cool in the oven with the door ajar. This stops the cheesecake cracking on top – a cunning tip from Gretchen.

When it is cold, you can take it out and serve straight away, or leave it in the refrigerator, where it will happily reside for up to 2 days.

Not granny's chocolate steamed pudding

This is one of those honest steamed puddings that goes down well with men who have been toiling all day and want something unsophisticated and filling. It makes them go all wistful and teary-eyed, telling you about their old granny who used to make the best steamed puddings. At which point, you beat them over the head with a wooden spoon and tell them that *this* one is pretty good too, actually, and there's yoghurt in the refrigerator if they'd rather ...

✳ Serves 4

125 g/4½ oz/⅔ cup (superfine) sugar
125 g/4½ oz/1 stick butter, softened
2 eggs
125 g/4½ oz/⅔ cup self-raising (self-rising) flour
1½ tsp cocoa powder (unsweetened cocoa)
50 g/1¾ oz/1¾ squares plain (bittersweet) chocolate, melted
½ tsp vanilla extract
1½ tsp milk

✳ *You will need a 1.2-litre/2-pint pudding basin and some string*

Grease the pudding basin generously.

Beat the sugar and butter together till pale and creamy and then slowly beat in the eggs. Add the flour and cocoa gradually and then beat in the chocolate, vanilla and enough milk to give a smooth mixture.

Pour the mixture into the basin, then cover the top with greaseproof (waxed) paper and tie with the string (just like granny used to do). I top the whole lot off with a layer of foil, but I don't know what granny would say to that.

Put a steamer over a saucepan over boiling water, then put the basin into the steamer and reduce the heat to a simmer. Steam for 1–1½ hours – test the sponge after 1 hour and see how you go. A skewer will come out clean when it's cooked. Don't let the water boil dry.

This pudding really needs some sort of lubrication – chocolate custard, chocolate sauce (see p.109) or just a good puddle of pouring cream.

Perfect chocolate parfait

Though I say so myself, this is a humdinger. An ice cream, to all intents and purposes, that requires no churning, very little skill (hoorah!), and tastes of chocolate heavenliness. I love the fact that you slice this and so don't have to struggle with a spoon that bends as you try and chip bits off a great brick.

✳ Serves 8

3 large eggs, separated
500 ml/18 fl oz/generous 2 cups
    double (heavy) cream
150 g/5½ oz/¾ cup caster
    (superfine) sugar
50 g/1¾ oz/½ cup cocoa powder
    (unsweetened cocoa)
200 g/7 oz/7 squares plain
    (bittersweet) chocolate,
    chopped into fine pieces

✳ *You will need a small*
    900 g/2 lb loaf tin

First, line the tin (pan) with clingfilm (plastic wrap). Whisk the egg whites in a large, scrupulously clean bowl until stiff.

In a second bowl, whisk the cream until firm. Don't over-whip, but it does need to hold its shape.

In a third bowl, whisk the egg yolks and sugar together until really pale and thick. Then add the cocoa and whisk in too. Take a spatula or a big metal spoon and carefully fold in the egg white, a third at a time. When they are incorporated, fold the cream in. I find it easier to add the cream in stages, rather than all in one go.

Take a third of the chopped chocolate and sprinkle it on the base of the loaf tin. Add a layer of the cocoa mixture. Add more chocolate chunks and then keep layering until you reach the top. There are no hard and fast rules about how many layers you need.

Cover the top of the loaf tin with clingfilm and freeze for at least 12 hours.

Remove the parfait from the freezer 15 minutes before you want to serve it. Simply tip it onto a plate and remove the clingfilm. To cut, use a sharp knife dipped in hot water.

Chocolate bread and butter pudding

This is a world away from the hideous bread and butter pudding I used to have at school. This pudding is creamy, chocolatey and rich, and it makes you sigh with pleasure.

✱ Serves 6

4 large eggs
50 g/1¾ oz/¼ cup caster
    (superfine) sugar
275 ml/9 fl oz/scant 1¼ cups
    full-fat (whole) milk
275 ml/9 fl oz/scant 1¼ cups
    double (heavy) cream
1 vanilla pod (bean)
100 g/3½ oz/3½ squares plain
    (bittersweet) chocolate, broken
    into chunks
4 soft white bread rolls
soft butter
4 tbsp apricot jam (jelly)

Preheat the oven to 150°C/300°F/Gas Mark 2.

Whisk the eggs and sugar lightly. Put the milk and cream into a saucepan. Split the vanilla pod (bean) with a sharp knife and scrape out the seeds. Put the seeds and the pod into the pan. Heat the milk mixture until it comes up to boiling point, then remove from the heat. Add the chocolate to the pan and stir until it has melted.

Slice the bread rolls horizontally into about four slices and butter them liberally. Layer the bread in an ovenproof dish.

Add the chocolate milk mixture to the egg and sugar mixture, then whisk well. Pour through a sieve (strainer) into a jug (pitcher) and then pour over the bread. Press down on the bread to make sure it is all submerged.

Put the dish into a roasting tin (pan) and pour boiling water two-thirds of the way up the sides. Carefully place into the oven and cook for 20 minutes, or until the custard has set. You want a bit of a wobble still – don't overcook it.

Take the pudding out of the tin and let it cool. When it is cold, heat the apricot jam (jelly) in a small pan and strain out any large lumps. Brush the glaze over the pudding and leave to set. Eat at room temperature with cream.

Chocolate rice pudding

This has to be the ultimate in comfort food. A real winter warmer when hot, but surprisingly good cold – in which case, I think it needs serving in posh glasses and topped with grated plain (bittersweet) chocolate.

✳ Serves 6

120 g/4¼ oz/generous ½ cup pudding (short-grain) rice
1 litre/1¾ pints/4 cups full-fat (whole) milk
300 ml/10 fl oz/1¼ cups double (heavy) cream
100 g/3½ oz/½ cup caster (superfine) sugar
2 tbsp cocoa powder (unsweetened cocoa)

Preheat the oven to 150˚C/300˚F/Gas Mark 2.

Place all the ingredients into a heavy-based saucepan and bring to the boil, then pour into an ovenproof dish and pop into the oven. Cook for 1½–2 hours, or until the rice is cooked and you are happy with the consistency. Halfway through the cooking, give it all a good old stir.

Serve it up. Easy peasy.

Chocolate fondants

The cracking thing about this recipe is that you can make these fondants a couple of days in advance and they'll sit happily in the refrigerator till you are ready to cook them.

✳ Makes 8

185 g/6¼ oz/6¼ squares plain (bittersweet) chocolate, broken into pieces
185 g/6¼ oz/generous 1½ sticks butter, plus extra for greasing
3 large eggs
3 large egg yolks
6 tbsp caster (superfine) sugar
6 tbsp flour

✳ *You will need 8 dariole moulds or small pudding basins*

Preheat the oven to 200°C/400°F/Gas Mark 6. Grease the pudding basins generously.

Put the chocolate and butter in a heatproof bowl over a pan of barely simmering water. Don't let the bottom of the bowl touch the water. Leave alone until the butter and chocolate are melted. You can stir occasionally, but don't overdo it.

In a separate bowl, whisk the eggs, egg yolks and sugar until really pale and thick. Whisk in the melted chocolate mixture and then quickly fold in the flour.

Divide the mixture between the eight basins and place on a baking sheet. Bake for 8–10 minutes – you want a top that has a distinct crust, but a bit of a wobble underneath the crust. If you are unsure, stick a skewer in and make sure you've got a layer of cooked sponge before you hit the molten centre.

Once out of the oven, run a knife around each basin and then turn onto a plate. Add a few berries and a dollop of crème fraîche and serve immediately. Gorgeous.

By the way, if you are worried about turning out the puddings, don't. Just eat them straight from the basin.

Good old chocolate mousse

Just how many recipes are there for chocolate mousse? Thousands, probably. I don't know if this is the best one. All I know is that it is the mousse I always make, and I never have any complaints. I like serving it in tea cups with little biscuits (cookies) on the side, but pop it into ramekins, glasses or one big bowl. I have made it the day before serving, with no ill effects.

✳ Serves 6

225 g/8 oz/8 squares plain (bittersweet) chocolate
4 large eggs, separated
25 g/1 oz/⅛ cup caster (superfine) sugar
150 ml/5 fl oz/⅔ cup whipping cream

Melt the chocolate according to your preferred method, then leave to cool slightly.

Beat the egg yolks lightly and then whisk them into the chocolate a little at a time, until incorporated. Set aside.

In another bowl, whisk the egg whites and sugar together until you reach soft peaks. Whisk a third into the chocolate mixture and then gently fold in the rest, in two goes.

Whisk the cream to the soft peak stage and then carefully fold this in too. Carefully spoon the mousse into whatever receptacle you have chosen and stick in the refrigerator for at least 1 hour.

Do remember to take them out of the refrigerator at least 1 hour before you are going to eat them. The flavour is much better if they are not refrigerator cold, and the texture lightens up too.

Chocolate mousse cake

Oh hello, you sophisticated little number! Look at you there, looking all simple and un-fussed about with. But what darkness lies beneath? Something rather sinfully unctuous, that's what. This recipe is a classic example of why they tell you, "Don't judge a book by its cover". Plain at first glance – but one spoonful, and you are doomed. You can serve this with cream and some fruit, but it is lovely by itself.

✳ Serves 6

250 g/9 oz/9 squares plain (bittersweet) chocolate
4 large eggs, separated
110 g/4 oz/generous ½ cup caster (superfine) sugar
3 tbsp warmish water
cocoa powder (unsweetened cocoa), for dusting

Preheat the oven to 180°C/350°F/Gas Mark 4. Grease a 20 cm/8 in loose-based cake tin (pan) and then line the base with greaseproof (waxed) paper.

Melt the chocolate according to your preferred method, then let it cool slightly. Whisk together the egg yolks and the sugar until really pale and fluffy. (I use an electric whisk for this, but an ordinary one will do, though it will take a bit of time.) Carefully stir in the chocolate and the water.

In another bowl, whisk the egg whites until they form soft peaks and then fold them into the chocolate mixture, a third at a time.

Pour the mixture into the prepared tin and bake for 15 minutes. Take it out of the oven and leave it to cool, then chill in the refrigerator for at least 2 hours – overnight is better.

Take it out of the refrigerator 1 hour before serving. It slides out of the tin easily, but use a hot, wet knife to slice cleanly. Dust heavily with cocoa powder (unsweetened cocoa) for a sophisticated look.

Chocolate ice cream

This ice cream is rich, dark, smooth – and very dangerous if you are short on will-power. It is also a great base for serious tinkering: add chocolate chips, mint oil, coffee, pieces of honeycomb, a few raspberries – whatever takes your fancy.

* Serves 8

500 ml/18 fl oz/generous 2 cups milk
4 large egg yolks
125 g/4½ oz/generous ½ cup caster (superfine) sugar
100 g/3½ oz/3½ squares plain (bittersweet) chocolate
40 g/1½ oz/scant ½ cup cocoa powder (unsweetened cocoa)

Put the milk in a saucepan and bring to a boil. Meanwhile, melt the chocolate in a heatproof bowl over a pan of barely simmering water and then let it cool slightly.

Whisk the egg yolks and sugar together until really thick and pale; I use the electric mixer for this. While the mixer is still whisking the eggs and sugar, pour the hot milk slowly into the bowl. You can also do this by hand; just add the milk slowly and whisk really well between each addition. Whisk in the melted chocolate, followed by the cocoa.

Pour into a heavy-based saucepan and stir over a really gentle heat until the custard starts to thicken. It should coat the back of a spoon. Take it off the heat and let it cool down, then transfer the mixture to an ice-cream machine and churn according to the manufacturer's instructions.

If you don't have an ice-cream machine, never fear! Put the custard into a shallow plastic container and freeze. Every 30 minutes, take it out of the freezer and whisk well with a fork, to break up the big ice crystals. You can stop doing this when the mixture is firm and is becoming difficult to whisk.

One tip: take the ice cream out of the freezer 15 minutes before you want to serve it.

Chocolate sundae

You look at a pudding like this in a glass and you think, "That looks *gorgeous* but I'll order the lemon, polenta and seagrass panna cotta – I do want the sundae, but it's too shameful ..." I say, "Throw caution to the wind and stand up for your pudding rights!" Failing that, just stay at home, make yourself a sundae and relish the entire thing, knowing that someone, somewhere is gnawing their way through a sophisticated, yet ultimately disappointing pudding, wishing they'd had the guts to order the sundae.

❋ Serves 1

a small handful of raspberries
2–3 scoops of chocolate ice
    cream (p.44)
3 chocolate digestives, crushed
    into chunks (p.93, though
    bought digestives are
    acceptable too)
1 tbsp of hot chocolate sauce
    (p.109)
1 tbsp whipped cream
wafer-type biscuit or
    chocolate finger

❋ *You will find this pictured
on p.29*

Get a lovely sundae glass that will hold an appropriately large amount. Place a few raspberries at the bottom of the glass. Add a scoop of ice cream and follow this with some crushed biscuits and a drizzle of chocolate sauce. Repeat until you reach the top of the glass, then adorn your work with a dollop of whipped cream. Squirty cream is entirely unacceptable here. A drizzle of sauce and a wafer biscuit or a chocolate finger stuck in at a jaunty angle finishes the whole thing off – apart from the maraschino cherry, of course, and the cocktail umbrella, the small sparkler, the extremely long spoon ...

Lady Hélène's roulade

Helen is my right-hand woman. She has noted that her station in life is due a bit of an upgrade, so, by the powers invested in me (by me), she is now to be known as "Lady Hélène". Having been given this recipe for her famous roulade, I am in no position to refuse her anything. It's a classic.

* Serves 8

175 g/6 oz/6 squares plain (bittersweet) chocolate
6 large eggs, separated
175 g/6 oz/scant 1 cup caster (superfine) sugar

For the filling
75 g/2¾ oz/2¾ squares plain (bittersweet) chocolate, melted
300 ml/10 fl oz/1¼ cups double (heavy) cream, whipped
strawberries, chopped
cocoa powder (unsweetened cocoa) and icing (confectioner's) sugar for dusting

* *You will need a swiss roll tin (jelly roll pan) measuring about 33 x 23 cm/13 x 9 in*

Preheat the oven to 180°C/350°F/Gas Mark 4. Grease and line the swiss roll tin (jelly roll pan). Melt the chocolate using your preferred method, and cool.

Whisk the egg yolks and the sugar together until pale and fluffy. Add the melted chocolate and whisk in too. In another bowl, whisk the egg whites until stiff and then fold into the chocolate mixture in three batches. Pour the mixture into the prepared tin and bake for about 15 minutes.

Remove from the oven, and leave to cool. Now for the crucial bit: place a clean, dry dish towel over the top of the cooled cake. Then place a damp dish towel on top of the dry one and leave to stand for at least 8 hours, or overnight.

Get a sheet of baking parchment (parchment paper) and sprinkle it with icing (confectioner's) sugar. Turn the cake onto the sheet of sugary paper and peel off the lining paper. Trim each of the short ends and make them nice and neat.

Spread the melted chocolate over the cake, then quickly spread over the whipped cream and sprinkle with the strawberries. You need to get this rolled up before the chocolate sets – stop dawdling. From the long end, start rolling up the cake, using the paper to help you. When you have rolled it all up, place on a serving plate with the seam at the bottom and dust with a mixture of cocoa and icing sugar.

Rather posh chocolate chestnut terrine

This is one of my small repertoire of sophisticated puddings. The chestnut purée appeals to adult tastes, and the tartness of the dried cranberries alongside the boozy lumps of amaretti biscuits (cookies) really makes it quite festive. It's a great alternative to Christmas pudding actually – but don't keep it just for Christmas. That would be wrong. I like to serve this with a dollop of crème fraîche, and a few chestnuts, either crystallized (candied) or that have been sitting in a jar of something unctuous.

✳ Serves 12

4 tbsp Amaretto liqueur
175 g/6 oz amaretti biscuits (cookies), broken into large chunks
500 g/1 lb 2 oz/18 squares plain (bittersweet) chocolate
200 g/7 oz chestnut purée (unsweetened)
600 ml/1 pint/2½ cups whipping cream
200 g/7 oz/2 cups dried cranberries

Line a 900 g/2 lb loaf tin (pan) with clingfilm (plastic wrap).

Drizzle the Amaretto over the amaretti biscuits and leave to one side.

Melt the chocolate according to your preferred method.

In another bowl, stir the chestnut purée into the melted chocolate. Lightly whip the cream to the soft peak stage. Take 2 tablespoons of the cream and beat it into the chocolate and chestnut mixture to loosen it up a bit. Then carefully fold in the rest of the cream. Next fold in the crushed amaretti biscuits (cookies) and the cranberries.

Spoon the mixture into the prepared tin and smooth the surface. Cover with more clingfilm and stick it in the refrigerator for at least 3 hours, or overnight.

It should turn out really easily onto a serving plate and you can remove the clingfilm. Cut with a hot knife for really smooth slices.

Chocolate "triffel"

I have no idea where it started, but trifle is always called "triffel" in our house. Strange name aside, this is all about the custard. It's gorgeous.

❋ Serves 10–12

For the sponge
75 g/2¾ oz/½ cup self-raising (self-rising) flour, sifted
25 g/1 oz/¼ cup cocoa powder (unsweetened cocoa), sifted
1 tsp baking powder
110 g/4 oz/generous ½ cup caster (superfine) sugar
110 g/4 oz/½ cup soft margarine
2 large eggs

For the custard
3 large egg yolks
50 g/1¾ oz/¼ cup caster (superfine) sugar
1 tbsp cocoa powder (unsweetened cocoa)
1 tbsp plain (all-purpose) flour
100 g/3½ oz/3½ squares plain (bittersweet) chocolate
150 ml/5 fl oz/⅔ cup milk
150 ml/5 fl oz/⅔ cup double (heavy) cream
1 tsp vanilla extract

4 tbsp kirsch
2 punnets raspberries
200 g/7 oz/scant 1 cup mascarpone

Preheat the oven to 180°C/350°F/Gas Mark 4. Line a baking tin (pan) with silicone liner or greaseproof (waxed) paper.

In an electric mixer, combine all the sponge ingredients and beat away until the mixture is light and moussey. Tip into the tin and bake for 25 minutes, or until springy to the touch and a skewer comes out clean. Leave to cool.

Next get on with the custard. Beat the egg yolks and sugar together in a large bowl, then add the cocoa and flour and carry on beating. Melt the chocolate using your preferred method. Pour the milk and the cream into a heavy-based saucepan and then heat. Once hot, pour it over the egg and sugar mixture, whisking continually. Pour the mixture back into the saucepan, then return it to the heat. Stirring constantly, bring the custard to the boil. When the custard has thickened, remove from the heat. Still stirring, add the melted chocolate and the vanilla. Pour the custard into a container and cover the surface with a layer of greaseproof paper – this stops a skin forming. Let it cool.

To assemble the trifle, get your nicest glass bowl. Break up the sponge and put a layer into the bottom of the bowl. Sprinkle the kirsch over the sponge. Tip the raspberries over the top and then carefully spoon the lovely custard over the fruit. Put the mascarpone into a bowl and beat it to loosen it up, and then spoon onto the custard. Cover the bowl and chill the trifle for 1–2 hours. Remember to take it out of the refrigerator at least 30 minutes before serving.

White chocolate panna cotta

Looks lovely, tastes lovely, feels lovely. Bliss.

✳ Serves 6

4 sheets gelatine (gelatin)
500 ml/18 fl oz/generous 2 cups
  double (heavy) cream
150 ml/5 fl oz/⅔ cup milk
1 vanilla pod (bean)
100 g/3½ oz/3½ squares white
  chocolate, broken into chunks
25 g/1 oz/⅛ cup caster
  (superfine) sugar
white chocolate curls and a few
  red berries, to decorate

Place the gelatine (gelatin) leaves in a shallow dish and cover with water. Set to one side.

Pour the cream and milk into a heavy-based saucepan. Take the vanilla pod (bean) and split it lengthways with a sharp knife. Scrape out the seeds and put them into the pan with the milk and cream and add the scraped pod too. Bring to boiling point and then remove from the heat. Add the chocolate and the sugar to the pan and stir until the chocolate has dissolved.

Take the gelatine and squeeze out the excess moisture, then pop it into the pan. Keep stirring until the gelatine has dissolved and all is smooth and gorgeous. Then strain the mixture into a jug (pitcher) and leave to cool to room temperature. Pour the liquid into six ramekins or dariole moulds and put into the refrigerator for at least 6 hours.

You may choose to eat the panna cotta straight from the ramekin or you may want to turn them out. If you do, loosen the puddings by dipping the pots in warm water before up-ending onto a plate and giving it a good hard tap on the bottom. (Cheeky.)

Decorate with a few chocolate curls and a berry or two.

Chocolate and hazelnut meringues

Amazing. Make a huge pavlova, tiny meringues or whopping, billowy pillows.

❋ Serves 6

For the meringue
6 large egg whites
300 g/10½ oz/1½ cups caster
  (superfine) sugar
1 tbsp cocoa powder
  (unsweetened cocoa)
1 tsp red wine vinegar
150 g/5½ oz/1 cup hazelnuts,
  roasted, skinned and chopped,
  plus extra for dipping

200 g/7 oz/7 squares plain
  (bittersweet) chocolate

For the filling
400 ml/14 fl oz/1¾ cups double
  (heavy) cream
1 tbsp caster (superfine) sugar
2 tbsp cocoa powder
  (unsweetened cocoa), optional

Line two large baking sheets with silicone liners. Preheat the oven to its lowest setting, whatever that might be.

Whisk the egg whites until stiff. Sprinkle the sugar onto the egg whites a spoonful at a time and whisk between each addition. Sift the cocoa over the mix, then sprinkle on the vinegar and the hazelnuts and fold it all in very carefully.

If you are making a pavlova, simply spread the mixture over the two baking sheets. For individual meringues, put the mixture into a piping (pastry) bag, fitted with a plain nozzle (tip), and pipe meringues, the size you want, onto the sheets.

Put the meringues into the oven for at least 3 hours. When they are hard on top and you can tap them lightly, turn the oven off and leave them in the oven until it is completely cold.

Melt the chocolate according to your preferred method. Dip the bases of the individual meringues into the chocolate, and then into the chopped hazelnuts. Leave to set before filling.

To make the filling, lightly whip the cream and sugar together until soft peak stage. Sift the cocoa over the cream and carefully fold it in. Don't overly sweeten. Add more cocoa if you want a darker, more bitter finish or leave the filling plain. Sandwich two meringues together with a blob of cream, or spread one layer of pavlova with the cream before putting the top layer on and dusting with icing (confectioner's) sugar.

Pastries & breads

3

A good chocolate tart is as fine a dessert as a good lemon tart. Fact. Pastry and dough seem to have an affinity with chocolate. Even if you consider yourself a calamitous baker, I implore you to try some of these recipes. I confess that, for a long time, if I saw "yeast" listed in the ingredients of a recipe I turned the page. One day, I have no idea why, I bought a box of yeast sachets and had a go. What a revelation! Making dough-based goodies is really therapeutic. And, what's more important, not half as complicated as it sounds. True, you have to build in time to leave the dough to prove and then bash it down, then do it all over again. But you can get on with all sorts of other jobs while waiting for the dough – shopping online for shoes, for example.

Pastry is not hard. There are just a few rules, and if you follow them, you will make lovely pastry. Resting it in the refrigerator is crucial, as is using the right ingredients. If I can do it, you can. It's not about skill. It's about having a go.

The best chocolate tart in the world

Probably. Everything a chocolate tart should be: simple, rich and smooth.

❋ Serves 8

For the pastry
175 g/6 oz/1½ sticks butter
75 g/2¾ oz/¾ cup icing
    (confectioner's) sugar
2 large egg yolks
225 g/8 oz/1½ cups plain
    (all-purpose) flour

For the filling
2 large eggs
3 large egg yolks
50 g/1¾ oz/¼ cup caster
    (superfine) sugar
150 g/5½ oz/1¼ sticks butter
200 g/7 oz/7 squares plain
    chocolate (70% cocoa solids),
    broken into chunks

First make the pastry: put the butter, icing (confectioner's) sugar and egg yolks into a food processor and blitz it, then add the flour and blitz again until you have a smooth paste. Tip the whole lot onto a sheet of clingfilm (plastic wrap) and work into a ball. Chill it in the refrigerator for at least 1 hour.

Preheat the oven to 180°C/350°F/Gas Mark 4. Roll out the pastry and line a 25 cm/10 in tart tin (pan). Cover with greaseproof (waxed) paper and baking beans (pie weights) and bake blind for 25 minutes, or until pale golden in colour and cooked through.

Take the case out of the oven and turn up the heat to 190°C/375°F/Gas Mark 5.

For the filling, beat together the eggs, egg yolks and sugar until really thick and fluffy – I do this in an electric mixer. Melt the butter and chocolate in a bowl over a pan of simmering water, taking care that the bottom of the bowl doesn't touch the water. When it has all melted, stir to combine, then take it off the heat and let it cool slightly. Pour the chocolate mixture over the egg mixture and briefly beat until all is thoroughly combined. Tip the whole lot onto the pastry case and bake for 5 minutes. Remove from the oven and leave to cool. Perfection.

Pear, almond & chocolate tart

Not only is this delicious, but it looks impressive and the constituent parts can be made days in advance, which is handy. A word about pears: Eddie Izzard has noted that they are an obtuse fruit. They sit in the fruit bowl, hard as stone for days on end. You turn your back, they ripen, and the next thing you know, they've turned to mush. So for this recipe, tinned or bottled pears are fine.

✱ Serves 10, or makes 4–6 individual tarts (halve the filling quantities for this option)

For the pastry
175 g/6 oz/1½ sticks unsalted butter, softened
50 g/1¾ oz/¼ cup caster (superfine) sugar
250 g/9 oz/1 ⅔ cups plain (all-purpose) flour, sifted
pinch of salt
1 large egg yolk
1 tbsp cold water

For the filling
250 g/9 oz/2¼ sticks unsalted butter, softened
250 g/9 oz/1¼ cups caster (superfine) sugar
25 g/1 oz/generous ⅛ cup plain flour, sifted
2 tbsp cocoa powder (unsweetened cocoa)
(continues above right)

First make the pastry: cream the butter and sugar together until light and fluffy. I do this in an electric mixer. Then beat in 1 tablespoon of the flour, followed by the salt and the egg yolk. Add the remaining flour, 1 tablespoon at a time. When it is all incorporated, add the water and give it a final mix. You will end up with a lovely, smooth, pasty dough. Tip it onto a sheet of clingfilm (plastic wrap), then wrap it up and place in the refrigerator for at least 1 hour, or until you need it.

Take it out of the refrigerator and roll it out to fit a 25 cm/ 10 in flan tin (pan) – I like to roll it out a bit larger so there are edges of pastry flapping over the top. (Alternatively, split the pastry between small individual tartlet tins.) Cover the pastry with greaseproof (waxed) paper and weigh down with baking beans (pie weights). Place it on a baking sheet and put it back in the refrigerator for at least 20 minutes.

Preheat the oven to 200°C/400°F/Gas Mark 6, then bake the pastry for 15 minutes, or until pale golden brown and cooked through. Remove from the oven.

250 g/9 oz/1⅔ cups ground
   almonds
4 large eggs
2 tsp chocolate extract (optional)
4 large, or 5 medium, ripe dessert
   pears
3 tbsp apricot jam (jelly)
100 g/3½ oz/3½ squares plain
   (bittersweet) chocolate

✳ *You will find these pictured on
   p.55 (prior to decoration)*

Reduce the oven temperature to 160°C/325°F/Gas Mark 3.

For the filling, cream the butter and sugar together until
pale and fluffy – again, I use the electric mixer. Beat in the
flour, cocoa and 2 tablespoons of the ground almonds until
lovely and smooth. Add the eggs one at a time and beat away,
then add the chocolate extract if you are using it. Finally
fold in the remaining almonds. At this stage, I have success-
fully put the mixture into a container and stored it in the
refrigerator for a couple of days with no ill effects at all.

Carefully peel the pears, then halve and remove the cores.
I like to brush them with a little lemon juice to stop them
browning, but it's up to you. Spoon the chocolate and
almond filling into the pastry case and smooth it out.
Then place the pears on top and press down very gently;
you don't want to submerge them completely.

Bake for 45 minutes–1 hour, or until risen and golden, and
a skewer comes out clean. Remove from the oven and leave
to cool in the tin.

Warm the apricot jam (jelly) in a saucepan and strain out the
lumps. Then brush the glaze all over the top of the tart and
leave to set.

Finally, melt the chocolate and use a teaspoon to drizzle
lines of chocolate over the top of the tart.

Chocolate meringue pie

Lemon meringue pie – now, *there's* a dessert just asking to be adapted. Lemon and chocolate? No. Chocolate and orange? Now we're talking. Crisp, buttery pastry; a rich, dark chocolate and orange curd; fluffy meringue. Hello!

❋ Serves 8

For the pastry
175 g/6 oz/1½ sticks butter, softened
50 g/1¾ oz/¼ cup caster (superfine) sugar
250 g/9 oz/1⅔ cups plain (all-purpose) flour
1 egg yolk
1 tbsp cold water

For the curd
100 g/3½ oz/3½ squares plain (bittersweet) chocolate
2 large oranges, juice and zest
85 g/3 oz/scant ½ cup caster (superfine) sugar
juice 1 lemon
85 g/3 oz/¾ stick unsalted butter, cut into cubes
3 large eggs

For the meringue
3 large egg whites
150 g/5½ oz/¾ cup caster (superfine) sugar

First make the pastry by creaming the butter and sugar together until really pale and fluffy. Add 50 g/1¾ oz/⅓ cup of the flour and beat well. Then add the egg yolk, and once that is incorporated, add the rest of the flour. I find it easier to do all of this in a food mixer, but it's up to you. Add the water if necessary to bring the whole mixture into a ball of dough.

Place the mixture onto a sheet of clingfilm (plastic wrap) and wrap it up, then put it in the refrigerator for at least 2 hours.

For the curd, melt the chocolate according to your preferred method, then leave to cool. Put the orange zest and juice, sugar, lemon juice and butter into a wide pan and slowly heat, without letting it come to the boil. When all the sugar and butter has melted and dissolved, beat the eggs and add them, stirring all the time. Don't let the mixture get too hot and don't stop stirring! You don't want scrambled eggs. After about 10 minutes, the mixture will thicken. Take the pan off the heat and quickly beat in the cooled, melted chocolate. Keep beating until all the ingredients are well combined and then pour into a jar or bowl and put it in the refrigerator.

After the pastry has rested, roll out the pastry to fit a 20 cm/ 8 in loose-bottomed cake tin (pan). Put the pastry into the tin, then cover with greaseproof (waxed) paper, and weigh this down with baking beans (pie weights). Put the tin back into the refrigerator for 15 minutes.

Preheat the oven to 200°C/400°F/Gas Mark 6. Then bake the pastry for 15–20 minutes, or until it is golden at the edges and cooked on the base. Let it cool for a minute or two.

Meanwhile, make the meringue. Whisk the egg whites until they form stiff peaks. Slowly add the sugar and keep whisking between each addition.

Take the curd out of the refrigerator and spoon it into the bottom of the pastry shell. I don't use all of the curd – it keeps well in the refrigerator for up to 2 weeks – but it's up to you how much you use. Then spoon or pipe the meringue over the curd. Pop it back in the oven for 20–25 minutes, or until the top of the meringue has crusted over and is look-ing golden and delectable. Remove from the oven.

This is best eaten cold – just warm if you really can't wait. It's gorgeous the next day too...

Chocolate mince pies

Bitterness is the key here. I know it sounds wrong, but mincemeat is so sweet that 100% cacao is the perfect foil (100% cacao is quite widely available but, if you can't find it, use the most bitter chocolate you can find). You will have some mincemeat left over; put it in a jar and store in the refrigerator.

❋ Makes 12

For the chocolate pastry
50 g/1¾ oz/scant ½ stick butter
50 g/1¾ oz/scant ¼ cup lard or white vegetable fat (shortening)
200 g/7 oz/1⅓ cups plain (all-purpose) flour
25 g/1 oz/¼ cup cocoa powder (unsweetened cocoa)
25 g/1 oz/⅛ cup caster (superfine) sugar
1 large egg yolk
1 large egg, beaten, for egg wash

For the mincemeat
100 ml/3½ fl oz/scant ½ cup apple juice
100 g/3½ oz/½ cup (solidly packed) soft dark brown sugar
450 g/1 lb cooking apples, peeled, cored and chopped
100 g/3½ oz/⅔ cup currants
100 g/3½ oz/⅔ cup sultanas (golden raisins)
50 g /1¾ oz/½ cup flaked (slivered) almonds
1 tsp ground cinnamon
1 tsp allspice
½ tsp ground cloves
50 g/1¾ oz 100% cacao, grated

First make the pastry: in a food processor, blitz the butter, lard (shortening), flour, cocoa and sugar until the mixture resembles fine breadcrumbs. Add the egg yolk and blitz again. If the dough does not come together, add cold water 1 teaspoon at a time. When you have a ball of dough, wrap it in clingfilm (plastic wrap) and pop it into the refrigerator.

Put the apple juice and the sugar into a big saucepan and heat until the sugar has dissolved. Add the remaining ingredients and gently bubble away for 25–30 minutes, or until the apples have cooked and you have the most wonderful, dark, fragrant mixture. Be careful that it doesn't stick to the pan. If you need to add more apple juice, do so.

Preheat the oven to 180°C/350°F/Gas Mark 4 and take the pastry out of the refrigerator. Give it a quick knead on a floured surface and then roll out until about 3 mm/ ⅛ in thick. Cut out circles and place them into a greased 12-hole bun tin (pan). Re-roll the remaining pastry and cut out 12 small stars. Put a teaspoonful of mincemeat into each pastry case and top with a pastry star. Brush a little bit of egg wash onto the star and then bake in the oven for 15 minutes, or until the pastry is crisp.

Delicious hot, with ice cream, or brandy butter, or cold.

Chocolate millefeuille

Right, let's get this over with from the start: I do not make puff pastry. The stuff you buy is infinitely better than anything I could make. If you are a whizz at puff pastry, be my guest. I applaud you, but you won't catch me making it. If you can, get the really buttery sort, it's the bee's knees. The recipe itself is a doddle. Enough said.

✳ Serves 6

plain (all-purpose) flour for
    dusting
600 g/1 lb 5 oz puff pastry
1 large egg yolk
100 g/3½ oz/3½ squares plain
    (bittersweet) chocolate (at least
    70%), smashed into gravel-
    sized pieces
300 ml/10 fl oz/1¼ cups double
    (heavy) cream
100 g/3½ oz/3½ squares milk
    chocolate, smashed into gravel-
    sized pieces
100 g/3½ oz/3½ squares white
    chocolate, smashed into gravel-
    sized pieces

Preheat the oven to 180°C/350°F/Gas Mark 4 and line a baking sheet with greaseproof (waxed) paper or a silicone liner.

On a flour-dusted work surface, roll out the pastry to approximately 40 x 25 cm/15 x 10 in – don't get too hung up on exact measurements. Then cut the pastry into 24 rectangles, by cutting into four along the short end and six along the long side.

Lightly beat the egg yolk and brush six of the rectangles with the egg – these will be the tops of the millefeuille.

Bake for 20 minutes, or until golden and puffed. Transfer to a wire rack to cool. Melt the plain (bittersweet) chocolate, according to your preferred method. Once it has melted, take it off the heat and whisk in 100 ml/3½ fl oz/scant ½ cup of the cream. Repeat this process with the milk and the white chocolate, so that you end up with three bowls of ganache.

To assemble, place a pastry rectangle on a plate and spread one-sixth of the plain chocolate ganache carefully over it. Top it with another pastry and add one-sixth of the white chocolate ganache, pop on another pastry and add some milk chocolate ganache and then top with a glazed pastry rectangle. Repeat. That's it.

Profiteroles

Hands up who doesn't love these? Not difficult and just made for scoffing. Make them as big or as small as you like. Personally, I can't think of anything nicer than a pillow-sized profiterole.

✳ Serves 4

For the choux buns
50 g/1¾ oz/scant ½ stick butter
60 g/2¼ oz/generous ⅓ cup plain (all-purpose) flour
2 large eggs, lightly beaten
150 ml/5 fl oz/⅔ cup water
150 ml/5 fl oz/⅔ cup double (heavy) cream, whipped to soft peaks

For the chocolate sauce
1 tbsp butter
2 tbsp golden (corn) syrup
100 g/3½ oz/3½ squares plain (bittersweet) chocolate

Preheat the oven to 220°C/425°F/Gas Mark 7. Line two baking sheets with baking parchment (parchment paper) or silicone liners.

For the choux buns, put the butter and the water into a saucepan. Heat until the butter has melted and then bring to the boil. Take it off the heat and immediately tip in the flour, then beat vigorously with a wooden spoon until the mixture forms a ball in the middle of the pan. Put the pan back on the heat and keep beating until the mixture is really smooth. Remove it from the heat and let it cool for a moment or two – you don't want to scramble the eggs that you are about to add.

This is the moment when I pour the mixture into a food processor, but you could carry on beating by hand. In a slow stream, add the eggs, while the food processor is running or while beating vigorously. The mixture will develop a lovely sheen.

With a piping (pastry) bag, pipe small balls onto the baking sheets, allowing space between each bun. Alternatively, just spoon the mixture onto the sheets. Bake for 20–25 minutes, or until risen and golden.

Remove from the oven and lower the temperature to 180°C/350°F/Gas Mark 4.

Make a small hole in the side of each bun with a skewer or a knife to let the steam out. Return to the oven for 5 minutes, then take them out again and place on a wire rack to cool.

Make the chocolate sauce by melting the butter, syrup and chocolate over a low heat, stirring now and again. When everything has melted, it is done. Easy.

To fill the buns, it really is easiest to use a piping bag. Fit a medium plain nozzle (tip) to the bag and fill with the cream. Find the steam hole you made earlier and use this to inject cream into the interior.

Pile all the profiteroles onto a lovely dish and pour the molten chocolate all over. Alternatively, take your one, massive, pillow-sized profiterole into a quiet corner and sink yourself into it.

Chocolate buns

Two small words and one big recipe: these buns are heavenly, but not to be tackled if you are in a rush. That said, your kitchen will smell dreamy and your labours will be duly honoured by the gratitude and fulsome praise of all those you allow to share these buns.

✳ Makes 20

For the dough
600 g/1 lb 5 oz/4 cups strong white (white bread) flour
100 g/3½ oz/½ cup caster (superfine) sugar
½ tsp salt
3 sachets (envelopes) easy blend (active dry) yeast – 21 g/¾ oz in total
100 g/3½ oz/⅞ stick butter
400 ml/14 fl oz/1¾ cups milk
2 large eggs

For the filling
150 g/5½ oz/1¼ sticks butter, softened
150 g/5½ oz/¾ cup caster (superfine) sugar
2 tsp cocoa powder (unsweetened cocoa)
100 g/3½ oz/½ cup plain (bittersweet) chocolate chips
1 large egg, beaten

For the glaze
3 tbsp apricot jam (jelly)
2 tbsp water

✳ *You will need a tin (pan), approx. 38 x 28 cm/15 x 11 in*

Line the tin (pan) with silicone liners or baking parchment.

Mix the flour, sugar, salt and yeast in a large bowl. Melt the butter and add it to the milk and the eggs and give it all a good whisk, then pour it over the flour mixture. Get your hands in and mix it all up, and when it is combined place it on the work surface. Knead until the dough is really smooth and elastic. Shape it into a ball and put it in a bowl, then cover with clingfilm (plastic wrap) and leave it in a warm, draught-free place for about 30 minutes.

After this time, the dough will have risen. Take it out of the bowl and cut off one-third of the ball. Stretch this out to fit the base of the baking tin. Roll out the rest of the dough, on a lightly floured surface, until you get a rectangle approx. 50 x 25 cm/20 x 10 in. Don't be too alarmed by the measurements – this is just a guide.

For the filling ingredients, mix the butter, sugar and cocoa in a bowl. Spread this mixture over the rectangle of dough, then sprinkle the chocolate chips over, as evenly as you can. Roll up the dough from the longest side until you have a very impressive sausage of dough, then cut 2 cm/½ in slices off the sausage. Place the slices on top of the base dough and brush the tops of the buns with the beaten egg. Cover with clingfilm and leave in a warm area to prove once more.

(continues overleaf)

This will take 20–30 minutes: the buns will have puffed up and will be jam-packed next to each other in the tin.

Preheat the oven to 230°C/450°F/Gas Mark 8. Bake the buns for 20–25 minutes, or until golden and risen. Remove from the oven and leave them in the tin.

For the apricot glaze, put the jam (jelly) and water in a saucepan and heat until the jam has melted. Strain the mixture, to remove the lumps of apricot, and then brush the glaze over the still warm buns. Serve immediately.

Chocolate and prune bread

This is a proper loaf of bread. Not cake. Bread. Lovely with butter, warm from the oven, and also really nice the next day, toasted. If you like the idea of making something doughy, choose this loaf of loveliness. You won't be disappointed.

✱ Makes 1 large loaf
   or 2 small loaves

3 sachets (envelopes) easy blend
   (active dry) yeast – 21 g/¾ oz in
   total
2 tbsp caster (superfine) sugar
625 ml/21 fl oz/2½ cups warm
   water
1 kg/2 lb 4 oz strong white (bread)
   flour, plus extra for dusting
30 g/1 oz/1½ tablespoons salt
250 g/9 oz/generous 1 cup ready-
   to-eat (no-soak) prunes,
   roughly chopped
250 g/9 oz/9 squares plain
   (bittersweet) chocolate, chopped

In a jug (pitcher), dissolve the yeast, sugar and half of the warm water.

Pop the flour and salt into the biggest bowl you've got and make a well in the centre. Add the yeast and water mixture and stir all the liquid into the flour. I like to do this with my hands; it is so much easier.

Slowly add more and more of the warm water until you have a lovely dough. Sometimes you may need a little more water, and sometimes a little less – all flours are different.

Place the dough out onto a floured work surface and start kneading it. Fold it over on itself and push it out away from you. Really get the heels of your hands in there and give yourself and the dough a bit of a work-out. You will notice that the dough gets smoother and smoother and more and more elastic. When you have been kneading for about 5 minutes, knead in the prunes and the chopped chocolate, trying not to break up the additions too much.

Form the dough into a ball and score the top with a knife. Put it into a bowl and cover with clingfilm (plastic wrap) and then put the bowl somewhere warm and away from draughts. Leave it for 45 minutes, or until the dough has doubled in size.

Grease a loaf tin (pan), or two tins, then dust with flour. Take the dough out of the bowl and bash it about a bit to knock the air out. Then place the dough into the tin and leave the dough to prove – it will double in size again.

Preheat the oven to 200°C/400°F/Gas Mark 6 and bake for 45–50 minutes. The loaf will sound hollow when tapped on the bottom. Don't worry about taking it out of the tin before it's finished cooking – you can pop it back in the oven out of its tin. It won't mind at all.

Cool on a wire rack.

Cakes & cookies

4

You must know that this chapter means business. After all, you can't beat a good bit of chocolate cake. Whether it's a loaf cake; a simple sponge, layered with cream and jam (jelly), smothered in buttercream; or some sort of indulgent fudgy concoction, there's a cake to suit all tastes, budgets and time restraints.

And when I talk about a basic chocolate cake, I mean that it is straightforward to make but tastes anything but basic. There are a few unexpected ingredients to add a certain twist to the proceedings, but please do not be frightened. My aim is to tickle your tastebuds, not leave you running for the hills and generally emotionally scarred by a culinary horror. That would be wrong.

When it comes to biscuits and cookies, a chocolate addition to the tin is always welcome, and quite frankly, a cinch to make. Word of warning, though: they may not stay in the tin long and then you'll have to make more ... and more ... and more ...

Basic chocolate cake

This is a cake to make when you have people coming to tea and you want to impress but don't have the time or inclination to take any risks or expend any effort with twiddles and twirls. The combination of chocolate and blackcurrant is gorgeous. The cake looks lovely and is one of those recipes that you can pull out when you don't know what else to do. It is the cake equivalent of the little black dress.

✳ Serves 8

150 g/5½ oz/1 cup self-raising (self-rising) flour, sifted
25 g/1 oz/¼ cup cocoa powder (unsweetened cocoa)
175 g/6 oz/scant 1 cup caster (superfine) sugar
175 g/6 oz/¾ cup soft margarine
3 large eggs
1 tsp vanilla extract
200 ml/7 fl oz/generous ¾ cup double (heavy) cream
2 tbsp blackcurrant jam (jelly)
icing (confectioner's) sugar, for dusting

Preheat the oven to 180°C/350°F/Gas Mark 4. Butter and line two 20 cm/8 in cake tins (pans) with greaseproof (waxed) paper.

In a mixer, food processor, or large bowl with an electric hand whisk, beat together the flour, cocoa, sugar, margarine, eggs and vanilla until light brown and really fluffy. (I said it was basic.)

Split the mixture between the two tins and smooth out. Bake for 25 minutes, or until the cake top is springy to the touch and a skewer stuck into the middle of the cake comes out clean.

Turn the cakes onto a wire rack to cool and remove the greaseproof paper.

When the cakes are cold, whisk the cream until it reaches soft peaks. Try not to overwhip it. Spread the jam (jelly) over one of the cakes and then top with the cream. Place the other cake on top and dust the very top with icing (confectioner's) sugar.

Chocolate fudge cake

If you are after a rich, moist chocolate cake with a fudgy, truffle-y icing, then this is the bad boy for you.

* Serves 8

175 g/6 oz/1¼ sticks butter, softened
350 g/12 oz/1¾ cups caster (superfine) sugar
1 tsp vanilla extract
3 large eggs
175 ml/6 fl oz/¾ cup milk
5 tbsp sour cream
75 g/2¾ oz/½ cup plain (all-purpose) flour, sifted
150 g/5½ oz/1 cup self-raising (self-rising) flour
100 g/3½ oz/1 cup cocoa powder (unsweetened cocoa)
2 tbsp Nutella, or other chocolate spread

For the icing
200 ml/7 fl oz/generous ¾ cup double (heavy) cream
200 g/7 oz/7 squares plain (bittersweet) chocolate (70% cocoa solids), broken into gravel-sized pieces

* *You will need a 20 cm/8 in loose-based cake tin (pan)*

Preheat the oven to 180°C/350°F/Gas Mark 4. Butter and line the cake tin (pan) with greaseproof (waxed) paper.

In a large bowl, beat the butter, sugar and vanilla together until light and fluffy. Add the eggs, one at a time, beating well between each addition. Now add the milk and sour cream and beat away. You will think it's curdled, but don't worry! Sift over the mixture both the flours and the cocoa, then fold in. Pop the mixture into the tin, smooth it down, and make a slight dent in the centre of the cake with the back of a spoon. Bake for 1 hour, or until a skewer poked into the middle of the cake comes out clean. You may need to cover the top of the cake with baking paper (parchment paper) for the last 10 minutes or so, if it looks like the top is burning. Remove the cake from the oven and leave to cool for 10 minutes in its tin, then turn onto a wire rack to cool.

Prepare the ganache for the icing. Heat the cream in a heavy-based pan until just below boiling point. Take it off the heat and let any bubbles die away, then tip in the chocolate and stir gently until it has all melted and you are left with a shiny ganache. Leave to cool and thicken for 10 minutes.

Cut the cake horizontally through the middle and sandwich together with the Nutella. Place the cake on the wire rack over a tray. Pour the ganache over the whole cake, then use a palette knife (spatula) to spread it all over the top and round the sides. Leave it well alone to firm up and set for at least 1 hour before serving.

Mum's brownies

Please be aware of the honour that is being bestowed upon you. My mother makes excellent brownies. She puts chopped nuts in hers – I don't. Up to you. They're delicious either way.

✳ Makes about 16

110 g/4 oz/1 stick butter
50 g/1¾ oz/1¾ squares plain (bittersweet) chocolate (70% cocoa solids), broken into large chunks
2 large eggs, lightly beaten
225 g/8 oz/1⅛ cups caster (superfine) sugar
50 g/1¾ oz/⅓ cup plain flour, sifted
1 tsp baking powder
100 g/3½ oz/⅔ cup chopped nuts (optional)
pinch of salt

Preheat the oven to 180°C/350°F/Gas Mark 4 and line a tin (pan) with greaseproof (waxed) paper. Leave the paper about 5 cm/2 in above the height of the tin, because the brownie rises before it falls.

Melt the butter and the chocolate in a heatproof bowl over a pan of barely simmering water – don't let the bottom of the bowl touch the water. When it has melted and is lovely and smooth, take it off the heat and let it cool slightly for a few minutes. Then add the remaining ingredients and beat well. Spread the mixture into the tin and flatten it out.

Bake for 30 minutes. The top should have crusted over, but the innards should still be moist. The brownie will continue to solidify as it cools. Have faith! There is nothing worse than an overcooked brownie.

Leave the brownie in the tin to cool before cutting and then transfer to a wire rack to cool completely.

Blondies

Well, if Mum's Brownies (p.78) are the classic brownie, then these are the great interlopers, coming up from behind and giving you a great big kiss on the chops. This is a recipe with a "more is more" approach. Nuts? Yes, bung them in. White chocolate? Oh, yes please. Chocolate chips too? Absolutely essential. I like to think of them as the Versace of the brownie world, darling.

✳ Makes about 16

110 g/4 oz/1 stick butter
250 g/9 oz/9 squares white
   chocolate, broken into chunks
2 large eggs, lightly beaten
50 g/1¾ oz/¼ cup caster
   (superfine) sugar
2 tsp vanilla extract
125 g/4½ oz/generous ⅔ cup
   plain (all-purpose) flour, sifted
100 g/3½ oz/generous ½ cup
   plain (bittersweet) chocolate
   chips
100 g/3½ oz/⅔ cup hazelnuts,
   roasted and chopped

Preheat the oven to 180°C/350°F/Gas Mark 4. Line a 20 cm/ 8 in square tin (pan) with greaseproof (waxed) paper, or a silicone liner, and leave about 5 cm/2 in poking up over the top of the tin.

In a heatproof bowl over a pan of barely simmering water, melt the butter and 125 g/4½ oz/4½ squares of the white chocolate. Don't let the bottom of the bowl touch the water. When it has melted, take it off the heat and stir in the rest of the white chocolate. Keep stirring. The residual heat will melt it. Leave to one side for a few moments to cool slightly.

In another bowl, whisk the eggs and sugar together until pale and thick. Add the chocolate and butter mixture, the vanilla and flour, then beat thoroughly but quickly. Add the chocolate chips and nuts and stir until evenly mixed.

Pour into the tin and smooth the top. Bake for 30 minutes, or until crusted and golden on top and still squidgy in the middle. Leave it all to cool in the tin, then cut into squares.

Beet the choccy cake

Before you turn your nose up at this, may I point out that dyed-in-the-wool beet haters (husband and son) have no trouble at all eating this like it's going out of fashion. I made this recipe into cupcakes and took a huge batch to my local farmers' market, and they positively flew! There is something deliciously satisfying about the rich and moist sponge, which is intensely chocolatey but with a fruity undertone. The chocolate cream cheese frosting isn't too bad, either.

✳ Serves 8

150 g/5½ oz raw beetroot (beet), grated
200 ml/7 fl oz/generous ¾ cup sunflower (corn) oil
250 g/9 oz/1¼ cups caster (superfine) sugar
3 large eggs, separated
3 tbsp milk
2 tsp chocolate extract (optional)
200 g/7 oz/1⅓ cups self-raising (self-rising) flour
1 heaped tbsp cocoa powder (unsweetened cocoa)
1 tsp baking powder

For the frosting
50 g/1¾ oz/1¾ squares plain (bittersweet) chocolate
250 g/9 oz/generous 1 cup cream cheese
300 g/10½ oz/3 cups icing (confectioner's) sugar, sifted

Preheat the oven to 170°C/325°F/Gas Mark 3 and grease and line two 20 cm/8 in cake tins (pans).

Take a small spoonful of the grated beetroot (beet) and pop it in a bowl and then just cover with boiling water. Set aside.

Whisk together the oil and sugar, then add the egg yolks, one by one, whisking well between each addition. Add the milk and the chocolate extract (if using) and carry on whisking. Stir in the remaining grated beetroot. Sift in the flour, cocoa and baking powder and fold that in too.

In another bowl, whisk the egg white until really stiff and then fold into the mixture in three batches.

Divide the mixture between the two tins and bake for 30 minutes, or until a skewer comes out clean. Leave the cakes in the tins to cool for about 5 minutes, then turn out onto a wire rack to cool completely.

To make the frosting, melt the chocolate according to your preferred method, then leave to cool. Put the cream cheese

(continues overleaf)

and icing (confectioner's) sugar into a big bowl and beat well until smooth. Add the melted chocolate and stir it in.

From the bowl containing the beetroot and water, take 1 teaspoon of the intensely coloured liquid and add it to the frosting. If you find that this has made the frosting too runny, add a bit more icing sugar.

When the cakes are cold, take about one-third of the frosting and sandwich the two cakes together. Then use the remaining frosting to cover the top and the sides of the cake. A palette knife (spatula) will make your life much easier here. Decorate the cake with chocolate sprinkles, Maltesers or a bit of grated chocolate. Not necessary, but always welcome.

Leave the cake for 1-2 hours before serving.

Chocolate brandy cake

I used to work in a magical café in Exeter. Sadly, it doesn't exist anymore. There was a gaggle of us girls who used to whip up concoctions amid much laughter and scandalous gossip. This refrigerator cake was a café favourite. It is delicious and easy, freezes well, and always hits the spot. Who could ask for more?

✳ Serves 12

250 g/9 oz/9 squares plain (bittersweet) chocolate
225 g/8 oz/2 sticks butter
3 large eggs
75 g/2¾ oz/generous ⅓ cup soft light brown sugar
225 g/8 oz digestive biscuits, crushed
175 g/6 oz/generous 1 cup raisins, soaked in 3 tbsp brandy for 1 hour
100 ml/3½ fl oz/scant ½ cup double (heavy) cream
100 g/3½ oz/3½ squares plain (bittersweet) chocolate, chopped into pieces

✳ *You will find this pictured on p.73*

Line the base of a large flan dish, preferably one with a removable base.

Melt the chocolate and butter together in a heatproof bowl over a pan of barely simmering water. Don't let the bottom of the bowl touch the water. When melted, set to one side.

In a very large bowl, whisk the eggs and sugar together until really pale and fluffy. (It really pays to go for it here: use an electrical whisk and save your arms.) When you are happy with the pale fluffiness, add the chocolate and butter mixture, the crushed biscuits and the raisins and any brandy still sloshing in the bottom of the bowl. Stir well to combine.

Pour the mixture into the lined dish and smooth it out and press down slightly with the back of a spoon. Cover with clingfilm (plastic wrap) and then either pop it straight into the freezer for another day, or stick it in the refrigerator for about 3 hours to firm up. About 1 hour before serving, take it out of the refrigerator and pop onto a serving plate.

Heat the cream in a heavy-based saucepan. Remove from the heat just before it comes to the boil, then add the chocolate. Stir until the chocolate has melted and you have a lovely, smooth, shiny ganache. Pour over the top of the cake and leave to set. Yummy. (If you prefer a plainer cake, simply dust with icing (confectioner's) sugar instead.)

Chocolate Guinness cake

At the market the other day, I met a man who said he didn't like chocolate. Determined not to let this pass, I started telling him about Chocolate and Guinness cake. Well, I changed his mind.

Serves 8

110 g/4 oz/1 stick butter, softened
275 g/9½ oz/generous 1⅓ cups (solidly packed) light soft brown sugar
2 large eggs, lightly beaten
200 ml/7 fl oz/generous ¾ cup Guinness
175 g/6 oz/scant 1¼ cups plain (all-purpose) flour, sifted
50 g/1¾ oz/½ cup cocoa powder (unsweetened cocoa)
1 tsp bicarbonate of soda (baking soda)
½ tsp cream of tartar

Preheat the oven to 180°C/350°F/Gas Mark 4. Line a 450 g/1 lb loaf tin (pan) – I use one of those ready-made fluted loaf liners.

Cream the butter and sugar until pale and fluffy and then beat in the eggs a little bit at a time. Add the Guinness and stir well. Add the flour, cocoa, bicarbonate of soda (baking soda) and cream of tartar. (I find it easiest to put all these dry ingredients into a sieve/strainer over the bowl and sift it straight into the bowl.) Carefully fold the dry ingredients into the wet and then pour into the prepared tin. Bake for 40–45 minutes, or until a skewer comes out clean. If the cake looks like it is getting a bit overdone on top, cover it with some greaseproof (waxed) paper while it finishes cooking.

I don't think this cake requires any form of icing – it is gorgeous just cut into manly slabs.

Chocolate "fondant" cupcakes

OK, I've cheated. So, for legal reasons, I've put the word "fondant" in quotation marks. When I say "fondant", what I actually mean is "Well, there's a gooey, chocolatey centre that is a bit like a fondant. But look, I'm trying to give you a delicious cake, OK? So don't go getting all cross and literal on me." Will that do?

✳ Makes 12

110 g/4 oz/½ cup soft margarine
85 g/3 oz/generous ½ cup self-raising (self-rising) flour, sifted
25 g/1 oz/¼ cup cocoa powder (unsweetened cocoa)
110 g/4 oz/½ cup caster (superfine) sugar
2 large eggs
1 tsp vanilla extract
12 heaped teaspoons of Nutella (or other chocolate spread)
icing (confectioner's) sugar, for dusting

Preheat the oven to 180°C/350°F/Gas Mark 4. Line a 12-hole muffin tin (pan) with cases.

In a large bowl, or preferably a mixer, put in all the ingredients apart from the Nutella. Whisk for 5 minutes, or until you have a light, almost moussey texture.

Divide the mixture between the 12 cupcake cases – don't worry about smoothing the surfaces, just plop it in. Bake for 15–20 minutes, or until firm on top, and risen and slightly springy to the touch.

Leave the cupcakes in the muffin tin for 2 minutes, then take a small sharp knife and cut out a conical shape from the top of each cupcake. Pop 1 heaped teaspoon of Nutella into each hole and put the lid back on. Press down gently, then sprinkle a tiny bit of icing (confectioner's) sugar over the top of each cake.

Serve while just warm, when the Nutella is still liquid and oozy. However, eating them cold is not a disaster, just texturally different.

Chocolate, date & banana bread

I have no idea why this is called a "bread". It isn't bread, it's definitely a cake – and a jolly good one at that. It is a loaf cake, so I suppose that might have something to do with it. Word of warning: don't try and cut it while it is still warm; it will fall apart. If you want it to be more chocolatey, add 1–2 teaspoons of cocoa to the mix. I don't think it particularly needs it, but tastes vary and who am I to tell you how much chocolate you need?

* Serves 8

3 ripe bananas, mashed
2 large eggs
100 g/3½ oz/½ cup (solidly packed) light soft brown sugar
120 ml/4 fl oz/½ cup sunflower (corn) oil
50 g/1¾ oz/scant ⅓ cup chopped dates
1 tsp vanilla extract
1 tsp ground cinnamon
275 g/9½ oz/scant 2 cups plain (all-purpose) flour
25 g/1 oz/½ cup wheatgerm
100 g/3½ oz/generous ½ cup plain (bittersweet) chocolate chips
1¼ tsp baking powder
¾ tsp bicarbonate of soda (baking soda)

Line a 900 g/2 lb loaf tin (pan), either with a liner or with a well-greased strip of greaseproof (waxed) paper along the base.

Beat together the bananas, eggs, sugar, oil, dates, vanilla and cinnamon. Then carefully mix in the remaining ingredients. That's it! Tip the mixture into the tin, then bake for 45–50 minutes, or until a skewer comes out clean.

Leave to cool on a wire rack.

Butterscotch chocolate chip cookies

This recipe came about after having a fiddle around with one of my all-time favourite cookie recipes. It's quick, it's easy and uses stuff that you generally have knocking around in the kitchen cupboard. A plan with no drawbacks.

✳ Makes one batch – you might make them huge, you might make them tiny...

125 g/4½ oz/generous 1 stick butter
175 g/6 oz/scant 1 cup (solidly packed) soft light brown sugar
1 large egg
1 tsp vanilla extract
150 g/5½ oz/1 cup plain (all-purpose) flour
½ tsp baking powder
200 g/7 oz milk chocolate chunks

Preheat the oven to 180°C/350°F/Gas Mark 4 and line two baking sheets with silicone liners.

Melt the butter in a large saucepan. Add the sugar and stir it around until the sugar has dissolved and the mixture starts bubbling, then take it off the heat immediately. Beat the mixture to cool it down a little, then add the egg, beating it in quickly. Add first the vanilla, then the flour and baking powder. Once everything is well combined, add the chocolate and give it another quick stir.

Take small spoonfuls of the mixture and plop them onto the baking sheet, leaving masses of room between each blob to allow for spreading. Bake for about 10 minutes. Leave the cookies on the baking sheet to firm up for a few minutes, then transfer to a wire rack to cool completely.

What-a-lotta-chocca cookies

Um. Yes. This recipe has appeared before. It featured in *Cookie Magic*, along-side a rather macabre, yet mouthwatering, photo of these beauties. But it *has* to be in this chapter too. It would be criminal to omit the most chocolately cookie on the planet (probably) from a book about chocolate. This recipe uses industrial quantities of chocolate. Brilliant.

✳ Makes one batch

125 g/4½ oz/scant 1 cup plain
   (all-purpose) flour
½ tsp bicarbonate of soda
   (baking soda)
25 g/1 oz/¼ cup cocoa powder
   (unsweetened cocoa)
125 g/4½ oz/4½ squares
   chocolate, 70% cocoa solids
85 g/3 oz/¾ stick butter, softened
175 g/6 oz/scant 1 cup (solidly
   packed) soft light brown sugar
2 large eggs
1 tsp vanilla extract
350 g/12 oz/2 cups milk
   chocolate chips
55 g/2 oz white chocolate chunks

Preheat the oven to 180°C/350°F/Gas Mark 4 and line two baking sheets with silicone liners.

Sift the flour, bicarbonate of soda (baking soda) and cocoa into a large bowl and set aside.

Break the plain (bittersweet) chocolate up and melt in a heatproof bowl set on top of a pan of simmering water – don't let the bottom of the bowl touch the water. Remove from the pan and let the melted chocolate cool slightly. Cream the butter and sugar together until pale and fluffy, and then beat in the eggs and the vanilla extract. Stir the melted chocolate into the mixture, followed by the milk and white chocolate. Fold the flour mixture into the chocolate mixture and then plop small spoonfuls onto the baking sheets. Leave room for spreading.

Bake for 10 minutes, then remove from the oven. Leave them on the sheets to firm up a bit, then transfer to a wire rack to finish cooling.

Safe as houses
chocolate digestives

The digestive is a homely, comforting, reassuring sort of biscuit. A chocolate digestive is all of the above but with the extra bonus that takes it from "everyday" to "wey-hey". Use milk or plain (bittersweet) chocolate – it doesn't matter. I would add, though, that there is a very good reason you don't get white chocolate digestives in the shops. Nasty.

✳ Makes one batch

100 g/3½ oz/scant ⅔ cup wholemeal (whole-wheat) flour
40 g/1½ oz/scant ⅓ cup plain (all-purpose) flour, plus extra for dusting
½ tsp baking powder
1 tbsp oats
120 g/4¼ oz/generous 1 stick butter, softened
100 g/3½ oz/½ cup (solidly packed) soft light brown sugar
4 tbsp milk
200 g/7 oz/7 squares milk or plain (bittersweet) chocolate

Preheat the oven to 190°C/375°F/Gas Mark 5 and line two baking sheets with silicone liners.

Mix the flours, baking powder and oats together in a large bowl. In another bowl, cream the butter and sugar together until pale and fluffy, then add the flour mixture to this. Add the milk a little at a time, until you have a thick dough.

Turn the dough out on to a lightly floured surface and give it a quick knead, until it's lovely and smooth, then roll it out to about 3 mm/⅛ in thick and cut into discs. Place the discs onto the baking sheets and prick them all over with a fork. Bake for 15 minutes, or until golden.

Transfer the biscuits to a wire rack to cool. When they are cold, melt the chocolate according to your preferred method, then spread the chocolate onto one side of the biscuit. Leave chocolate side up to set.

Biscotti with the choccolotti

These are delicious served with a creamy dessert – or even just a dollop of mascarpone, some raspberries and a glass of dessert wine. By the way, they keep for ages in an airtight tin.

＊ Makes one batch

125 g/4½ oz/generous ¾ cup whole almonds
100 g/3½ oz/3½ squares plain (bittersweet) chocolate, chopped into gravel-sized chunks
250 g/9 oz/1⅔ cups plain (all-purpose) flour
2 tbsp cocoa powder (unsweetened cocoa)
150 g/5½ oz/¾ cup caster (superfine) sugar
1 tsp baking powder
3 large eggs

Preheat the oven to 180°C/350°F/Gas Mark 4 and line two baking sheets with silicone liners. Chop the almonds very roughly – don't chop them too small.

In a large bowl, mix all the ingredients, apart from the eggs. Lightly beat the eggs, then stir them in until you form a cohesive ball of dough. I use my hands, which is much easier. If the dough is a bit too sticky, just add more flour until you are happy.

Halve the ball of dough and form it into two flat loaf shapes about 3 cm/1 in high and 20 cm/8 in long. Place the loaves onto the baking sheets and bake for about 20 minutes, or until cooked through. Remove the loaves and leave to cool. Do not turn off the oven.

When the loaves are cool, cut each into slices 5 mm/¼ in thick and place the slices back onto the baking sheets. Return to the oven for 10 minutes. Then take them out, flip them over and return to the oven for another 5 minutes. Transfer the biscotti to a wire rack to cool before putting them in an airtight tin.

Millionaire's shortbread

I love the idea of a bunch of millionaires sitting round, taking tea, discussing their pots of money, a cigar in one hand and reaching for their shortbread with another. They would certainly be discussing the legal position of prohibiting those with limited funds from eating such a delicacy. This shortbread *must* be consumed by millionaires only. What I want to know is, what do *billionaires* eat?

✳ Makes 12–24 depending on how you cut it

For the shortbread
250 g/9 oz/2¼ sticks butter, softened, plus extra for greasing
50 g/1¾ oz/¼ cup caster (superfine) sugar
250 g/9 oz/1⅔ cups plain (all-purpose) flour
125 g/4½ oz/scant 1 cup cornflour (cornstarch)

For the caramel
175 g/6 oz/1½ sticks butter
175 g/6 oz/scant 1 cup caster (superfine) sugar
4 tbsp golden (corn) syrup
1 x 400 g/14 oz tin (can) condensed milk

For the topping
350 g/12 oz/12 squares chocolate (milk or plain/bittersweet)

Preheat the oven to 170°C/325°F/Gas Mark 3. Line a 28 x 20 cm/11 x 8 in tin (pan) with silicone liner.

First make the shortbread. Cream the butter and sugar together until pale and fluffy. Stir in the flour and cornflour (cornstarch) and combine till you have a smooth, pasty dough. Press the mixture into the tin, squishing it right to the edges and getting a smooth surface. Prick with a fork and then bake for 20 minutes, or until pale golden brown. Leave in the tin to cool.

For the caramel, put the butter, sugar, syrup and condensed milk into a heavy pan and slowly, over a gentle heat, melt the mixture, stirring frequently. Once it has melted, bring it up to a gentle bubble and keep stirring. Do not stop stirring and be aware that the molten bubbling mass will spit at you when you are least expecting it. After about 5 minutes, it will be thicker and golden. Carefully tip the caramel over the shortbread. Leave for about 30 minutes to set a bit.

Melt the chocolate, then pour it over the caramel and place the shortbread in the refrigerator for 1–2 hours. When the chocolate has set, carefully cut it into squares as big or small as you want – don't forget, it's for millionaires, so it's rich. Try not to cut your beloved silicone liner.

No mucking around
chocolate macaroons

I am not known for my willingness to hold back on culinary extras. Plain and simple is anathema to me. When I started experimenting with a recipe for chocolate macaroons, I anticipated that I would sandwich them together with a rich ganache for a gloriously over-the-top treat. Well, I made the macaroons (about 20 times before I was happy, but you needn't lose any sleep over that ...) and then the strangest thing happened. They were just so lovely as they were that, for once, I decided to leave well alone. Feel free, though, to sandwich the little lovelies together with something glorious. I will understand.

✳ Makes 24

2 large egg whites
1 tbsp caster (superfine) sugar
75 g/2¾ oz/generous ⅔ cup
  ground almonds
2 tbsp cocoa powder
  (unsweetened cocoa)
125 g/4½ oz/1¼ cups icing
  (confectioner's) sugar, sifted
½ tsp almond extract
24 almonds

Line two baking sheets with silicone liners; the macaroons will stick to anything else. The only other alternative is edible rice paper. Preheat the oven to 180°C/350°F/Gas Mark 4.

In a large, clean bowl, whisk the egg whites until they form soft peaks. Then add the caster (superfine) sugar and whisk again until the mixture is really stiff and shiny. Fold in the ground almonds, cocoa, icing (confectioner's) sugar and the almond extract. Put the mixture into a piping (pastry) bag fitted with a plain nozzle (tip). Pipe small circles onto the baking sheets with lots of space between each blob, and pop an almond on top of each one. Bake for about 10 minutes, or until set and golden.

Transfer to a wire rack to cool. Crispy the first day and then deliciously chewy after that.

Drinks & sauces

5

A chocolate drink is sometimes just what the doctor ordered. Cold, miserable days, when one is feeling a little bit sorry for oneself, can be immeasurably improved by a cup of hot chocolate. A child, I have found, can be bribed into good behaviour with the promise of a chocolate milkshake, especially if they are allowed to help make it.

I have, for the first time in this book, used drinking chocolate in some recipes – the type that needs milk added. The same goes for the malted milk powders. But you do want to avoid those just-add-water instant drinking chocolates. No, no, no! They are far too thin and watery, and the results will be no good. A bad day may be made even worse.

One recipe that everyone needs is for chocolate sauce. A pudding emergency can be resolved with ice cream from the freezer and a quickly whipped-up sauce. Suddenly, you are a culinary hero and your guests are impressed because they know that, in the same position, they would have got a half-empty, sticky, squeezy bottle of something revolting out of their cupboard.

Bribery milkshake

I can't say that I employ this method of child-rearing often, but it has its uses. The occasional treat like this seems perfectly reasonable to me. I like that it certainly contains less sugar and weird ingredients than commercial versions.

* Serves one good boy with a
  large glass

2 tsp drinking chocolate
300 ml/10 fl oz/1¼ cups semi-
  skimmed (low-fat) milk
1 scoop chocolate ice cream
  (p.44)
4 ice cubes

* *You need a blender for this*

Mix the drinking chocolate with 2 teaspoons milk, then mix until smooth. Put all the ingredients into the blender (or use a hand-held blender) and blast away until smooth, with a lovely frothy top.

Pour into a large glass. I think it is probably written in some statute book that this must be drunk through a straw. Pat child on head and tell them what an angel they are.

Malted chocolate milkshake

This is excellent for sporty types who require readily absorbable energy. If you do stick it in a flask to take trackside, just remember to give it a good shake before pouring it out. And put it in a flask that will keep it cold.

* Enough for 2 large drinks

2 tsp drinking chocolate
4 tsp malted milk powder (such
  as Ovaltine)
1 litre/1¾ pints/4 cups semi-
  skimmed (low-fat) milk
1 banana, sliced
2 tbsp natural (plain) yoghurt
6 ice cubes

Mix the drinking chocolate and the Ovaltine with a little milk till smooth. Put all the ingredients into a blender and blitz away. That's it.

Moccachoccachino

This sounds like a fiddle, but it really isn't. The combination of coffee and chocolate is brilliant. You get the caffeine hit and bitterness from the strong coffee, tempered by the sweetness and smoothness of the hot chocolate. You do need one of those milk-frothing devices for this. If you don't have an espresso machine, make two small cups of very strong real coffee.

✳ Serves 2

4 tsp drinking chocolate
4 shots espresso coffee
500 ml/18 fl oz/generous 2 cups
    milk
plain (bittersweet) chocolate, for
    grating on top

Stir the drinking chocolate into the hot coffee. When it has dissolved, divide between two large cups or mugs.

Heat the milk to just below boiling point and then whisk until you have a lovely head of frothy milk.

Pour the milk over the coffee chocolate mixture, ensuring that both cups have a good dollop of froth on top. A minor stir will mix the milk into the mocha mixture.

Top with grated plain (bittersweet) chocolate.

Simply delicious
hot chocolate

Called "simply delicious" because it is simple and delicious. In Roald Dahl's *Charlie and the Chocolate Factory*, Augustus Gloop falls into a river of molten chocolate. Wow! This recipe is as close as you might get to that without the risk of drowning.

❋ Serves 2

500 ml/18 fl oz/generous 2 cups milk
200 g/7 oz/7 squares milk chocolate, broken into chunks

Simply pour the milk into a heavy-based pan and add the chocolate. Slowly heat the milk and chocolate, stirring frequently to stop anything sticking to the base of the pan. When the chocolate has melted and the milk is nearly boiling, it is ready. Pour into deep bowls and behave like a French school child and slurp from the bowl. Oh alright then, pour it into a mug. Spoilsport.

The more is more approach to hot chocolate

This is not a hot chocolate for puritans. If something can be added, add it. Needless to say, this can be tinkered with and bits left out or even more added. This is the only recipe on earth I can think of where squirty cream is acceptable.

✳ Serves 2

4 tsp drinking chocolate
600 ml/1 pint/2½ cups milk
50 g/1¾ oz/1¾ squares milk
   chocolate, chopped into
   chunks
1 can squirty cream

Optional toppings
2 tsps mini marshmallows
2 tsp flaked (slivered) almonds,
   toasted
2 chocolate flakes

First make a paste with the drinking chocolate and 2 teaspoons milk, then blend with the rest of the milk in a heavy-based saucepan. Add the chopped chocolate and heat slowly, stirring all the time. When the chocolate has melted and the mixture is just about to come up to the boil, take the pan off the heat and give it a quick blast with a hand blender, or use a balloon whisk.

Pour the chocolate into two heatproof glasses, or mugs. Top with a squirt of cream, and adorn as you wish. You could simply crumble a chocolate flake over the top or you could really go for it – sprinkle with marshmallows and toasted almonds, then plunge a chocolate flake into the cream with an extravagant flourish!

Chocolate martini

Oh dear, oh dear. The problem is that these are delicious. But don't have more than two. One is more than enough for me. These are more Bond Girl than 007. I can't really see James asking for a "chocolate martini, shaken, not stirred". You will need one of those snazzy cocktail shaker thingies and definitely a proper martini glass.

❋ Makes 1

1 tsp grated chocolate (100% cocoa solids)
ice cubes
50 ml/2 fl oz/¼ cup chocolate liqueur
2 tbsp vodka
raspberries, to garnish

First coat the rim of the glass by wetting it and then dipping it into the grated chocolate (you can also dip it into egg white for the same purpose). Put the glass in the refrigerator.

Put the ice cubes, chocolate liqueur and vodka into the shaker. Give it a good shake and then strain into the chilled glass. Top with a raspberry, either skewered onto a cocktail stick (toothpick) or just floating – as you wish.

Sticky chocolate sauce

This is the chocolate sauce that Mum used to make for us to go on top of ice cream. It's dark, sweet and rich, and goes all solidly chewy when it hits cold ice cream. It sets slightly when it cools too. Just re-heat to get it moving again.

50 g/1¾ oz/scant ½ stick butter
2 tbsp golden (corn) syrup
1 tbsp light soft brown sugar
2 tbsp cocoa powder
(unsweetened cocoa)

Put all the ingredients into a heavy-based pan and slowly heat. Stir constantly until it has all melted and is smooth and runny. Word of warning: hot sugary sauce means mouth-burningly hot. Let it cool for 5 minutes.

Slightly more sophisticated chocolate sauce

I say it's slightly more sophisticated only because it doesn't contain syrup and so doesn't have that extraordinary sticky sweetness. This sauce is great for pouring and is just the job for profiteroles or topping the steamed chocolate pudding on p.33.

200 g/7 oz/7 squares chocolate
(milk or plain/bittersweet or a
mixture of both), chopped
into chunks
25 g/1 oz/¼ stick butter
125 ml/4 fl oz/½ cup milk
1 tbsp double cream

Place the chocolate and butter in a heatproof bowl placed over a bowl of barely simmering water. Don't let the bottom of the bowl touch the water. Stir occasionally until the butter and chocolate have melted. Take the bowl off the pan and gradually whisk in the milk and then the cream. Place the bowl back over the pan to re-warm the sauce, whisking as you warm. Pour into a warmed jug (pitcher).

Index

Acknowledgements

Curiously, I had quite a number of people happy to test these recipes. I thank you all for your comments – you know who you are.

Emily, at Pavilion, in my opinion, deserves some sort of very high-ranking prize (accompanied by a very shiny medal on a pretty ribbon) for patience, tact, and the ability to have her work life made hugely complicated. Emily, thank you.

Thank you Lara and Monaz, for your incredibly hard work under duress!

To Polly, Beth and Tom, I say a huge thank you. The Pittmans rock! Charlotte – thank you for everything; Gretchen, Helen and Rosy for constant support and ideas; Mum for having some classic and brilliant recipes up her sleeve; and Tarek and Rory for being Tarek and Rory.